Romancing the Islands

Romancing the Islands

Journeys in the South Pacific

Kim Alan Gravelle

GRAPHICS (PACIFIC) LIMITED

SUVA   FIJI

The author wishes to thank Islands Business International for permission to reprint many of the stories in this book which first appeared in their in-flight magazines.
All photographs were taken by the author.

Colour Separations and pre-print filmwork were

prepared by Caines Scannertronics in Suva, Fiji.

ISBN: 982-214-002-9

This book is for Gudrun and Gabriel

Contents

Green Highways - An Introduction

I thought of calling this book Green Highways. That's because green, for me, is the epitome of islands, the thick verdant jungle that is common to most elevated islands, a solitary reason for putting up with all the things islands *don't* have. Of course, atolls don't have much green, but I've never wanted to be an atoll dweller. I like islands that look like little kids drew them, triangles poking up out of the deep blue sea.

Most of the islands in this book — in PNG, Fiji, Vanuatu, Tahiti, the Cooks — look like that. Green triangles rising out of the sea.

But 'highways' is a little misleading. Few of the island countries included in my Pacific travels have highways, and that is pure joy. I was looking at the word highways in an esoteric sense, a journeyer island-hopping on invisible pathways.

And the final reason I didn't call this book Green Highways is that I wasn't sure just how William Least Heat-Moon would take it. In a small van with a bed and a camp-stove, William Least Heat-Moon visited, stopped, talked to the people of back-roads America and wrote his conversations and encounters in a book he called Blue Highways.

I didn't start out to write this book. I just had a lot of stories I'd written about island encounters, most of them originally destined for newspapers and in-flight magazines. As Editor at various times of four Pacific-based in-flight magazines, *Polynesia, Royal Tongan, Solomons* and Air Pacific's *Islands,* I had opportunities to visit some pretty isolated environments, talk to whoever would listen, and push film through a couple of workable but beat-up Nikons.

Without realizing it, I was compiling material on the back-roads of the islands, so to speak. My daughter Gudrun sent me a copy of Blue Highways. She lives in Oregon where it's easy to buy a good book. It's a little harder in mid-Pacific. She knew I'd love it. And it gave me an idea...

Romancing the Islands is a collection of stories which, for the most part, were written in the last four or five years, most of them in the span between 1993 and the present. Some of the Fiji ones are only a few months old, some much older. I thought of 'modernizing' the book to bring all the stories up to date, but it would take much of the fun out of them. I didn't want to cross out all the people who, I knew, might no longer be there. The tin-can collecting priest in Niue has left the island. The police chief there has probably changed, and his pert Lieutenant in the tight blue skirt possibly melts fewer hearts these days. So what? They were — and are — part of the Pacific Parade. Many of the people encountered in these pages will still be just where they were when I found them. Some, like Greg Blanchette (Open Oceans, Open Boat) I'm frightened to ask about.

Likewise, some problems — Tonga's phone system, Tuvalu's lack of drinking water — are problems probably rectified by now. If they're not, well, this book is not meant to be a guidebook to anywhere. It's meant to convey the spirit of the islands, and that changes slowly, if at all.

As a time reference, of sorts, I can say that almost all stories on Tonga, the Solomons, Samoa, Tahiti, Niue, the Cooks and Vanuatu have been written since 1992. They were printed originally in *Solomons*, *Polynesia*, and *Royal Tongan* magazines, all published by Islands Business International in Suva.

Most of the Fiji stories are very current, three-quarters of them re-printed from Air Pacific's *Islands* magazine, excluding the two longest. *In the Wake of Bligh* was a Fiji Sun newspaper series, dating back to 1975, and the Rotuma story was first published by the Fiji Times in 1981. Rotuma now has an airstrip, and all the horrible things Rotumans imagined would happen with easy access to the world didn't, of course, ever happen.

A couple of other early Fiji pieces — *Mud Walking, A Stroll Across Viti Levu* and *Still Water, White Water*— are also Fiji Sun vintage. The Queensland story, *A Knife for the Heart*, was never published. It dates back to pre-1974, the year I moved permanently to Fiji.

I would like to express my appreciation to Islands Business International for allowing me to reprint stories which first appeared in their various in-flight magazines.

This book is for Gudrun and Gabriel, so that they can keep a record of what the old man was up to when he was wandering around, romancing the islands.

The *Bounty Launch* and the stony beach at Tofua in Tonga.

In the Wake of Bligh

My letter to Bill Verity came back this morning, undelivered. It bore an indelible stamp noting that there was no such person at that address. I thought of writing Clancy's Saloon on 3rd Avenue in Manhattan, but I wasn't really sure if there really was a Clancy's, or if it was just part of the Verity bravado, a name to go with one of his instantaneous stories. Verity, after all, could be anywhere: guzzling a beer in Clancy's, possibly, or at the bottom of the ocean, which is possible, too. It has been umpteen years since the zany, bearded fellow in a straw hat introduced me to the sea, ushered me across 800 kilometres of it in an open dinghy, and then dropped me off wharfside before continuing his re-creation of the epic 1789 voyage of Captain William Bligh.

Captain Bligh probably had fewer problems. At least initially.
When he and his 17 loyal crew members were cast adrift at Tofua, Tonga, a couple of centuries ago, they had few decisions to make. Just go, find land, survive.
Captain Bill Verity, re-tracing Bligh's 3,500 mile voyage from Tofua to Timor in an exact replica of the 'Bounty' launch, did not find things so easy. And it was mostly because of the wonders of the modern world: telephone calls that didn't go through, 16mm film that didn't arrive; an expense cheque from New York that

never came.

"I'm getting used to it," Bill Verity said, pounding a fist against his head. "I'm getting used to it, I'm getting used to it, I'm getting used to it ... "

Verity had just been to the Post Office in Nuku'alofa for the 500th time. No, they had said. Nothing yet.

What Verity wanted to see most was a medium size parcel with at least 2,000 feet of colour film. Enough at least to film the start of the voyage, the caves at Tofua where the Tongans had tried to stone Bligh's crew, the first 550 miles from Tofua to Fiji.

Leaving the Post Office, he had eyed a rounding collection of horse droppings and stomped squarely in the middle of it. It was obvious he was getting upset. A telephone call wasn't going to be the answer, either. The line, a radio link between Tonga and the outer world, seemed perpetually fully-booked. And it was about to close up for a three-day weekend.

"Heavy seas are nothing ... beautiful," he said. "But this kind of thing could drive somebody around the bend."

All around him, people kept smiling, nodding. "When you gonna' set sail, Cap'n Bligh?" they asked him. A lot of people were calling him 'Bligh' now.

Verity shook his head, vacantly staring at another horse dropping. "I shouldn't let it worry me." he said. "I should just settle down in beautiful Nuku'alofa and open up a television repair shop."

There is no television in Nuku'alofa.

Back at the hotel, a man who could play a ukulele with his toes was slowly losing his audience to some foxy looking ladies who were moving fairly dramatically on the disco floor. I had to forego the entertainment and head for bed. Tomorrow was going to be an unusually demanding day.

Long before breakfast, the short, bearded man in the odd floppy hat was pumping the bilge of the boat and singing something about a little grass shack. He was singing loudly.

To the people of Nuku'alofa, sitting idly along the slipway and observing an undeclared but pervasive rule of silence, more than the hat was odd. Even after three weeks in the Tongan capital, Bill Verity and the Bounty Launch lured clusters of the curious.

A church bell rang. In this tiny metropolis, a pealing bell is probably the most exuberant thing to ever happen. Or was, until Verity came.

Verity of the wine-soaked lunches and all-night gatherings; Verity writing love sonnets to the girls of Ma'ufanga; Verity — brash, sailorlike, his personality sparkling, electrifying everything around him.

If the Tongans thought Bill a curiosity, they could take solace in the fact that they were not alone. This modern day mariner is a password for a free drink from County Cork in Ireland to Clancy's Saloon on 3rd Avenue. And elsewhere.

The man who took a 12-foot boat across the Atlantic from Florida to Fenit, Ireland. Then reversed direction with a 20-foot copy of a Sixth Century Irish craft, the St. Brendan, and sailed it 5,800 miles from Ireland to the Bahamas through the infamous Devil's Triangle. The Irish seem to have a good grip on the Saint market.

Of course, Verity is actually American. Three hundred years worth, in fact, and all of the ancestors Long Island boat builders. If his family name and three years living in Ireland have lent a hint of Gaelic to his voice, well, it is still the Stars and Stripes that flies over his taffrail.

Beneath shading umbrellas, the Nuku'alofans were continuing their vigil. They knew 'Bligh' was in Tonga to retrace a historic voyage. And that he was going to do it in a 23-foot open boat. But few would know of his reputation as a damn fine navigator.

Or know that five years of research, studying Bligh's original charts and a British Naval Museum plan of the 'Bounty' launch had gone into what might appear to be little more than a lark. Every peg, every copper nail of that boat had been studied.

On Verity's walls in his Long Island home, blow-ups of Bligh's charts were everywhere. He could draw them in his sleep. Nor would the Nuku'alofans quite understand the intensity of the Verity experience that makes being alone a lifestyle.

"You reach a different level of intellect and association with your surroundings. I feel stronger, I have more stamina. I stay at this level for the entire voyage, every time I'm at sea, and it lasts maybe a week or two after I come ashore. Then I get involved with people, and I regret to say they are extremely annoying."

"Loneliness? I've been more lonely in the middle of Manhattan."

The journey in the St. Brendan had been the biggest test of that philosophy.

"I wasn't sure I could do it," he said. "I knew the boat could, but I didn't know how I would react. When I crawled up to the dock in the Bahamas, after 5,800 miles, I just went off by myself and sat on the edge of that dock. It was the greatest experience of my life."

The Nuku'alofans weren't the only ones watching Bill Verity.

I was watching him, too.

As a self-proclaimed landlubber, I had in a moment of madness agreed to trust my life to a man I'd met for one hour over a Suva Travelodge beer. A few of those beers had obviously dulled my usual quest for security. Yes, I had said, I'll come to Nuku'alofa and join you on that first segment of open sea.

It hadn't been encouraging, after the effects wore off, to hear chief officers of a British survey ship, HMS Hydra, say they wouldn't go out of Suva Harbour in an open boat. Regardless. Or later, to have Tongan sailors, good sailors and used to open boats, shake their heads.

The 'Bounty Launch' was 23 feet long with four wooden slats for benches, uncovered and totally exposed to the elements.

What magic, I pondered, could there be in a boat built in the lobby of a New York City skyscraper; an exhibition-piece nailed together as hundreds of rubber-neckers gawked? Even if it was built with traditional 18th Century tools and 300 years of boat building experience.

Verity was used to mad experiences: a motor-cycle racer, war time pilot and gunner, deep-sea diver, mercenary in the Israeli independence movement, graduate of the University of the World.

Alongside his experiences, mine paled: outright winner of a

savage fight with a frenzied coconut in New Guinea; the only person to paddle an orange fibreglass kayak the six miles from Bougainville to Shortland Island in the Solomons; scratched but left alive after an encounter with an amorous sea turtle.

Nothing, really, to compare.

Verity put my mind to rest. Let's go to lunch, he said. Four bottles of wine later ("I do all my hellraising on land," he admitted) we were toasting another turtle. Not the amorous one. This one was dead and stuffed in the window of Nuku'alofa's biggest hotel. It had been presented by Capt. Cook to the King of Tonga, and the hand-painted notice alongside it said the turtle had been burned by fire, kicked by a horse, and run over by an American Army jeep. Among other things.

Its name was Tui Malila, and the famous turtle graces Tonga's one cent coin.

I felt just as stuffed as Tui Malila did. Perhaps we both looked it, because the doorman was shaking his head. It seemed a lot of people in Tonga went around shaking their heads. "That man," said Verity, "hasn't stopped doing that since the night of the Prince's reception."

"Oh?" I said. Actually, I knew what he was going to tell me. I'd already heard it from others ... lots of others.

About how the Prince of Tonga had held a special reception with 200 guests to honour Bill Verity, and how Bill had spent all day at lunch with Tui Malila and gone looking for beche de mer and certain seaslugs to cure his hangover, and how he'd lost his shoes and socks and suddenly realized it was time to go to the reception, and how, the wine accenting his feelings of generosity, he had bought a large fish to give to the Prince, and how he arrived at the door with the dead fish tucked in his belt and his pants rolled up to his knees, eyes cheerfully dancing from the wine.

And how they had refused to let him in.

Someone started thumping a *lali* long, long before the sun came up. Almost in answer, prayers sung in falsetto voices floated across the beach and pounced into my Tongan *fale*.

Hiding didn't do any good. The booming of the wooden drum kept tempo with the throbbing in my head. Prayer, I thought, might indeed have its place. Lord save me from lunches like yesterday's. Vague recollections of Verity stepping from the surf starkers on some beach north of Nuku'alofa, gently caressing a large, rounded stone he was calling 'Martha'. Martha was bronzed and beautiful, almost certainly volcanic.

The sounds of prayer continued.

This unique little service on the wharf is performed for the benefit of those people travelling on the small, inter-island boats to other parts of Tonga. There are roughly twenty people per square foot on these boats, all crammed, jammed, pushed and packed into every available bit of deck space. Not to forget the bags of rice, taro tops and crated pigs. The prayer service makes good sense, all things considered. Somewhere in that throng, there might even be an ageing life jacket or two. The boat pulled out, a floating mass of waving hands, the waves gently nudging the Bounty Launch into motion. And then Verity started yelling, something about it being a good day for my trial run in the launch. "Euaiki", he said, as if that should explain it all.

Euaiki is the place where the shark people come from. They are the only people in Tonga who don't have to dress up when they visit the King, and who can present a shark as a gift, rather then a more succulent roast pig or crab feast.

What's all this monkey business about sharks? we asked Lopeti Tuitufu, a lad who comes from that island.

Long story, he said. But briefly:

"There were two men getting ready to leave Euaiki in their canoe, but as they started out, a third man was suddenly sitting in the middle. The two rowers went back for another bowl of kava and waited for the third man to leave. Which he didn't. So all three started out, the two men and the spirit. On the way to Tongatapu, the main island, a big shark circled the canoe. The spirit prepared to dive in the water and said, "If the blood in the water is light, it is the shark's blood and I have won. But if the blood is dark, the shark has won."

Lopeti looked very stern, particularly for a 17-year-old.

"The blood on the water was light and ever since, men from Euaiki need have no fear of the shark."

Now here is a bit of magic and wonder. Since then, Euaiki men go shark fishing with nothing but a rope. They jump out of their canoes, thrash around in the water to attract the creatures, tie a rope around the shark's head and drag them into the canoes.

"Bluff" I said. "No way." But later, mounds of steaming taro and fish spread before us, the villagers of Euaiki said yes, this is the way we catch the shark. No spears. "Unga has never bitten us," they say.

I secretly made a mental note of the shark's name. It is good to be on a first-name basis in a pinch. A little something to whisper in its ear.

Lopeti's father, Tevita, announced the arrival of 72-year-old Pita Tuitufu, a man who has really put the shark thing on the line. Pita is a legend in Euaiki.

Many years earlier, he was working on a tiny island called Toku with two other men. They ran out of food and had no boat. The copra boat wasn't due for weeks. Pita decided to swim for help — 48 miles away.

He swam for four days and five nights before he reached Falevai, and on the way, he encountered numerous sharks. On the morning of the third day, he decided he'd about had it. But then the spirit, the man in the canoe, told him to keep going. A little to the right. And so forth. And the vision saved him.

Tevita Tuitufu invited us to come with them in the evening and see for ourselves. We could swim with the sharks, he said.

Unfortunately, there were other things I had to do. Cut my toenails, for instance.

Sailing inter-island inside Tonga's reefs can be totally pleasant. My legs, if not exactly seamanlike, stayed more or less glued to the Bounty Launch and within the 7 by 23-foot limits I'd set for them. I could tell where they were at all times by the yellow rubber boots I was wearing.

From that brief jaunt, the trip to Euaiki, I decided that the Bounty

Launch and I were going to hit it off just fine. Which was good, because Verity said we would sail for Tofua on Monday. Sailing on Sunday — like fishing, ball-playing and almost everything else — is against the law in Tonga.

At the back of my mind, it seemed like we were still lacking a few essentials for the boat. Such as petrol for the small outboard motor that would take the place of Bligh's 17 rowing men if we had to fight our way off a reef.

Or boxes of delicious and exotic foods: whole canned pheasant cooked in Burgundy jelly, say. Or those French tins of lobster bisque.

"You sure we got everything?" I asked Verity cautiously.

"Hell yes," said the skipper.

It wasn't until later that I realized everything, for Bill Verity, is not necessarily everything.

Sunday morning, 'Bligh' looked carefully at the sky. He took off his hat, jumped once into the air, and shouted something. It sounded like "let's go."

We pulled out of the channel just as the police van arrived.

It was the start of the midnight watch, pitch black, no stars, and Verity had just shattered the absolute stillness with a piercing cry: "Just hold on, Norton, we're coming!"

John Norton was the Bounty crewman stoned to death at Tofua in 1789.

One hand on the small wooden tiller, the other flicking a torch on and off to check the course on the compass, I had the next three hours to contemplate just what was going on.

I was on a very small boat in a very wide sea. It was a long way sideways. The Bounty Launch, its gaff rigged sails occasionally luffing in a slack wind, was by Verity's description 'sea kind'. You'll never be in a more seaworthy boat than this one, he said.

I am not an authority on boats, but right from the start, I liked the looks of her.

She had magic, which is very important to me. I rarely do anything without considering the magic. And I could see she had one other thing: buoyancy. Buoyancy is almost more important then magic.

I also had the words of my grandfather, Matt Frasier, to reassure me. Fifteen years earlier, I had climbed aboard my first ship, a freighter bound from Boston to Liverpool, and had been somewhat nervous about it all. Don't worry, my grandfather had jokingly told me: "A lad born to be hung will never be drowned."

It was just before 3, time for Verity to take over; my eyelids were closing in rhythm with the waves, when suddenly the boat lurched. I thought we were aground in the middle of the sea, and then something smashed into it again. "Big fish," cried Verity. "Shark."

Gingerly, I tried voicing my well-rehearsed greeting: "Unga, darling, is that you?" This time, we could both glimpse a broad dorsal fin behind the boat. "Stop this silliness" I said, "and go back to Euaiki."

Unga, and I swear on my grandfather's tie that this is true, smiled, waved goodbye, and left. The shark, it seemed, had been attracted by the free-spinning prop of the tiny 5 HP outboard which was leaving a bright trail of phosphorescent light like a flashing fish's belly.

"Son of a gun gonna have one hellava toothache" was Verity's comment when later, in the daylight, he examined the damage: a bent prop, broken motor mount, a tooth-embedded chunk out of the rudder.

With the gray beginning of dawn, we could see a silhouette taking shape, the island of Nomuka. Nomuka has been a watering hole for mariners since Abel Tasman put it on his charts.

The 'Bounty' had been there with Bligh. So had Captain Cook.

The people of Nomuka did not seem especially surprised to see this strange little craft drop anchor off their beach. Curious faces peered over the side of the boat for about 15 minutes, and then adults and children went back to their marble games. Marbles are pretty big time in Nomuka. The only thing that can stop a marble game is when a horse and dray trots over the circle. Which happens all the time.

Verity was already stretched out under a tree, oblivious to the world. Or so it seemed. Until an inquisitive girl old enough to bear fruit gave him the eye.

"Fine, fine" Verity whispered from under his hat.

Nomukan girls don't seem to be as shy as the Nuku'alofans. Bligh's men probably changed all that. "You think you'll ever marry again?" I asked the hat.

"Do I look like I have any cerebral disorder that would make me join the realm of the living dead?" said the voice. The girl came a little bit closer, stretching out her toe to gently prod the sleeping figure.

"On the other hand," said Verity ...

Actually, it was all lies. This captain had already described, more than adequately, what he called the crabgrass syndrome, the weekend barbeques, the drivel at work about who was doing what to whom, the country-club rituals. He tired of it, became at one with the sea. Interviewers in New York called it 'self-denial'.

That is not what Verity called it.

"Pure goddamn glory" is what he called it.

We sailed out of Nomuka two hours after we came. I'd lost a blue star, a silver steeley, a chipped cat's eye and three green boulders. These people are hell on marbles.

What we DID have, finally, was some outboard motor oil, a minor oversight due to our unscheduled Sunday sailing. If anyone was to be critical of that outboard motor as an obvious deviation from doing things the William Bligh way, well, they'd be wise not to whisper it in Verity's ear. He has a special word for them. The wee outboard was good sense, considering he didn't have 17 people to row for him.

Somewhere a few miles off Nomuka, Verity began doing a strange sort of jig. He was pointing down to a patch of the briny that looked as gray and somber as any other chunk of sea.

"It was here," he said.

"Nice," I said.

"Stirring," said Bill. "It makes me old heart skip a beat."

"Uh, what?" I ventured.

"Where the mutiny was, of course!"

"Oh," I said.

April 28, 1789

Just before sun-rising, while I was yet asleep, Mr Christian, with the master-at-arms, gunner's mate, and Thomas Burkitt, seaman, came into my cabin and, seizing me, tied my hands with a cord behind my back, threatening me with instant death if I spoke or made the least noise...

Capt. William Bligh's 'Narrative of the Mutiny on the Bounty'.

Bligh and his men were allowed to collect sails, canvas, 28 gallons of water, 150 pounds of bread and a "small quantity" of rum and wine.

I'd been able to collect two bottles of port, which I was nursing in my arms like Naomi Campbell. (Yah, my first version of this story, in 1975, had the Pointer Sisters. Times have changed...). I socked another slug of port down and read Bligh's account of the Tofua experience.

My first determination was to seek a supply of breadfruit and water at Tofua and afterwards sail for Tongataboo, and there risk a solicitation to Poulaho, the King, to equip our boat and grant us a supply of water and provisions so as to enable us to reach the West Indies...

At dawn, we rowed along the shore in search of a landing place ... and discovered a cove with a stony beach at the NW part of the island ... about 150 yards from the waterside, there was a cave ...

But the landing was not without problems. Tonga at that time did not have a Tourist Bureau.

An attack began by about 200 men. The unfortunate poor man who had run up the beach was knocked down and stones flew like a shower of shot. Many Indians got hold of the stern rope, and were near hauling the boat on shore which they would have effected, if I had not had a knife in my pocket, with which I cut the rope ... at this time, I saw five of the natives about the poor man they had killed, and two of them were beating him about the head with stones ...

"You realize," Verity had said to me, "that for the film, you'll have to play Norton."

But I wasn't worried. Two hundred natives stoning me to death? I knew the time schedules of these enchanted isles. I knew that at least 199 of them wouldn't show up on time.

The island of Kau rose from the sea like a child's drawing of an island rising from the sea: a perfect cone. Tofua is right alongside, but much less perfectly shaped. A small canoe, paddled by one of the island's 60 inhabitants, was about to be pirated by Captain Verity. There weren't many options, as far as getting camera gear onto the beach.

The man in the canoe did not look like John Norton, proving beyond a shadow of doubt that Norton did not survive the attack and propagate the island with his children. The man in the canoe did not say 'Hello Bligh' or anything of the sort. He stared silently in disbelief as we threw him a rope. And towed him around to the northwest side of the island, Verity all the while scanning the shoreline for a cave and pebbled beach, which proved easy to find.

His due reward came in seeing the terror on my face during the canoe ride through the surf, Bolex movie camera and Nikon held above my head. If that wasn't enough, he really cracked up after my fourth step onto the beach. Those black lava stones, the ones they used to beat Norton with, were burning hot.

Certain Pacific islanders may think they have cornered the market on fire-walking. Not true. They have some new competition. My dance was less sophisticated, of course, but it worked: I almost never touched ground.

The man from the canoe was now having the best time he'd had in years. "Palangi feet" he said to me, smiling. I danced right past him.

'Bligh', in the meantime, landed, soaked but wearing shoes. He was wandering around in a state of spiritual reverence, hands held aloft, out-stretched, touching the stones, a dazed look in his eyes.

"Most beautiful thing to ever happen to me" muttered Verity.

Cameras safely back aboard the 'Bounty Launch' and 3,380 foot Kau disappearing in the distance, I was almost relieved to leave the ghost of Norton behind.

The sunrise was lovely and red the next morning. But what was that I remembered? Red sun in the morning, sailors take warning? An ugly cumulo-nimbus shaped like a giant red claw seemed to be reaching down toward the tiny boat.

From Capt. Bligh's Narrative of the Mutiny on the Bounty:

...at daybreak, the gale increased, the sun rose very fiery and red, a sure indication of a severe gale of wind...it blew a violent storm, and the sea ran very high, so that between the sea the sail was becalmed and when on top of the sea it was too much to have set...we were obliged to bail with all our might...I directed the course to the WNW so that we might get a sight of the islands called Feejee...

It began raining. A cold, drizzly rain. And the wind came up. "Now you'll see this little girl move," Verity said.

I didn't want to see it move. I wanted to see flat mill ponds and water lilies and frogs. I never met a frog or a water lily I didn't like.

The waves started to look rather high. To me, anyway. There was a sign on the top of one of them that read 'Sir Edmund Hillary was here'. Another sign said 'Sherpa guides for Hire.'

The rain started running down my sleeves, inside my nylon jacket. It continued to do that all day. It was still doing it at night: I could tell because I could see the waterfalls in my sodden wet sleeves by the light of the lightning flashes which were crashing just above my toes.

I took up religion. It was called the Reformed Church of Hard Ground and for communion, members have to eat a spoonful of dirt each month and worship trees and green things. The church's colours were green. I vowed that I would wander the countryside, preaching against sin and small boating.

From Bligh's log: *... in the evening, it rained hard, and we again experienced a dreadful night.*

From Gravelle's log: Ditto.

I wound myself around some protrusion to make as little a target for the lightning as possible. It was a very plausible mime of a tomato worm. Except that I was curled around a red petrol can instead of a real tomato.

In the morning, I pried open one eye very cautiously, just in case I was dead. There was another beautiful red sunrise.

But the day turned out to be much better than expected. If it hadn't been for the whales, it would have been a more or less average kind of a day.

Verity was the first to spot them, a large pod of Sperms blowing dead ahead. I looked at Verity to see what he was going to do, but he wasn't in the boat.

Only Captain Ahab was there.

"Bring the sail around," Ahab was yelling. We can catch those mothers."

The utter amazement of it all, seeing these creatures four or five times the length of the boat. And Ahab yelling that we can get closer.

"I had a whale's fluke trim my whiskers off the Grand Banks when I was crossing the Atlantic. Talk about halitosis. Damn thing blew all over me and the sails, and I couldn't get rid of the smell for weeks."

"Here he comes...only thing to worry about is if they're mating."

The Bounty Launch closed the gap. And then suddenly, the beasts disappeared. We were sailing right over their backs, and there were others all around us.

"Hey, look," screamed a demented Ahab. "They're mating."

We slid by unscathed. But later, we didn't seem to be sliding much at all. "Dream of fields of wheat blowing in the wind," said Verity. The Bounty Launch didn't seem to be going anywhere. Three knots, maybe, in a wind so light that the sails had to be set, bird winged and tied open with a pole.

"If anyone ever saw this arrangement," said the skipper, "I'd be drummed out of the business."

Still, it was a refreshing change from the wind and storm of the night before. We made 90 miles during the storm, the launch on a strong tack and moving like a skate. After the storm, she was plowing, not skating.

Bligh, in his log, talked about high seas and rain, the fatigue of bailing to keep the boat from filling. Verity's version had a bilge pump which made short work of the job. We also had a radar deflector and a sea anchor. Closing in on a reef at night or during the five hours a day that Verity planned to sleep during the long solo part of his journey, the sea anchor would be invaluable.

The Bounty Launch also had a plastic trash can full of tinned fish and Friendly Island biscuits. Verity was so fond of the combination that he could eat it three times a day. Worse, he imagined anyone else could. I would have happily paid a hundred dollars for a steak and green salad with a cold beer.

Bill must have caught my look of anguish. "Makes you appreciate life," he said, "when you can get your wet ass back in the middle of it."

That word reminded me of yet another problem. Sitting on a hard (ever so hard) wooden bench for six days had already done things to my scrawny anatomy never before accomplished. There is a member of the monkey family, a baboon I think, which has achieved a similar trade-mark. I casually mentioned the problem to the captain.

"Did I tell you about the time," he chimed in, "that I was sitting in Shorthall's Saloon with an ex-steeple-chase jockey and some lady comes in and introduces herself and said 'and what may I call you?' and I said 'call me anything but doctor — I need a holiday' and the lady said 'are you really a doctor?' And I groaned and looked dismayed and the Irish steeple-chase jockey said 'Lady, he's only the biggest damn gynecologist in New York City' and the lady said 'maybe you can help me'.

I was getting used to the Verity stories, to the dramatic pauses as his Volkswagen rolled down an Irish cliff, the fiddle player never losing a beat.

I also knew what he was going to say next, what the punch line was, so I spoiled his day and remained silent. He looked hurt.

A pterodactyl was floating overhead. I hadn't seen one for years. Or was it a frigate bird? Fijians always call them storm birds, but I associate them with good luck. Verity's bird is the Golden Headed Gannet which, he claims, has greeted him about 40 miles out on almost every landfall he'd ever made. I wasn't sure about a frigate bird's range, but I remember hoping this one was close to home.

The Lau Group was somewhere ahead. It could be on the horizon by the next dawn.

Verity had just completed a sextant reading ("holding a sextant in a small boat is just like riding a motorcycle on a washboard road: if you ain't got the technique, you're on the reef") and said we were somewhere close to where we were supposed to be. Amazing, considering one of the two helmsmen was a total novice at steering a course.

Bill had just mentioned a four-letter word. Reef.

Earlier, near the start of the voyage, he had made me listen to that sound. "Don't ever forget what it sounds like," he said. "It's going to be worth your life."

Now, unless we could catch sight of Moce, the island nearest our Lau Group entry, we were going to have to listen for that sound all night.

"Smell that," Verity said, craning his nose skyward.

"What?"

"Land. Sweet."

I could smell it now. In fact, with a little effort, I could smell cold beers, perfume, Golden Dragon ladies.

"A dog's brain is 70 per cent smell," Verity said.

"I can't smell a thing," I said.

At about 8 the next morning, Bill Verity's 19th boat, his very favourite, was sailing alongside the reef at Moce, looking for an opening. The reef sound I had been trying to hear all night was now freight-training through my head. Fifteen feet away, see-through green waves were smashing into the white froth.

"Might want to be a little further out," I suggested. And immediately got a lecture in return. "When I'm on this tiller, it's all business and I know what I'm doing."

Verity, intent, in charge.

But later, written in his log, I saw one word.

Hairy, it said.

In Bligh's narrative, it read:

...a little after noon, other islands appeared and at quarter past 3, we could count 8...I durst not venture to land as we had no arms and were

less capable of defending ourselves than we were at Tofua...

By noon, we too could count exactly eight islands.

Bligh had been chased off from 'Feejee' by war canoes. As we sailed past Moce, *takias*— traditional outrigger canoes with mat sails which have not changed in this part of the Lau Group since Bligh's time — came to the inside reef to watch us pass.

A strong current was sweeping into the Laus through the same hole we entered, pushing us along fast. Two hundred miles to go, a few islands and only one barrier reef this side of Suva Harbour.

"Couldn't have done it without this," noted the captain, pulling a tiny glass vial from his pocket. He said it was a present from the National Geographic Society, a copper nail plucked from the seabed off Pitcairn Island from HMS Bounty.

The final day's run was agony. Slow, hot and painful. The wooden bench was now ingrown.

Just after dusk, eight days after leaving Nuku'alofa, the lights of Suva were visible behind a long reef. And through a dense, cold rain.

Verity didn't have a harbour chart and was now reef dancing again, skirting the froth and looking for a channel he knew must be there. When two navigation lights, dead in line, suddenly appeared through the mist, we dashed for it, running a gamut of buoyed flashes, Verity cursing his way through the harbour.

It was absolutely coal black, the rain had drowned out the city's lights. But I knew I was home. Verity could have the next two months of solo travel, and the next 3000 miles. The thought of continuing on, past the Great Barrier Reef, past the northern end of Australia and possibly arriving in Timor was absolutely mind-boggling, a solo lunacy on tinned fish and an exposed, hard wooden bench.

We slid up alongside a big schooner, a 120-footer from America.

"Where's the yacht club?" we shouted out in the darkness.

"Where are you coming from?" said a soft female voice.

"Tonga."

There was a long silence.

"In that?"

Bill Verity continued his journey, alone as planned, and completed the voyage to Timor in the wake of Captain Bligh. William Bligh's journey took considerably less time than William Verity's, who suffered malnutrition and was hospitalized for a time on a small island off Cape York, Australia. He sold his hand-wrought, sea-kind boat for $400 to an island trader in Timor. When he returned to Fiji months later, it was with his new Tongan wife. They flew on to Manhattan.

Rotuma and Raho's Revenge

In the middle of Australia once, somewhere between Darwin and Tennant Creek, the bus driver had pulled to a stop. All around the bus, there was nothing to see - just a straight line on the horizon separating barren red dust from barren gray sky.

"Just out there," the driver had said, "is where Banjo Patterson wrote Waltzing Matilda. Do you want to take a picture of it?"

The absurdity of it all came back to me as I leaned out from the railing of the *Duiyabaki*.

I had reached my destination. Rotuma was apparently a stone's throw away, and yet I couldn't see it.

At 2 a.m., it just didn't seem to exist. There wasn't a silhouette or a sound, not the faintest hint of a kerosene lamp to indicate there was anyone or anything there.

I had been straining my eyes for an hour for some sign of life as ship's bells clanged and as we reduced speed until we were just perceptibly moving. The reward had been only the luminescent glow of waves breaking against the Duiyabaki's hull.

Captain Ted Lyson, Suva Harbourmaster who was putting in sea duty to bring the landing craft up, came out onto the bridge. "We're here," he said matter-of-factly, as if finding a dot in the Pacific, 300 miles from land on a starless night, was no small accomplishment.

"Looks lovely" I said, staring at the black void. But I knew it was there. I could smell it. There is a certain rich, pungently sweet smell I associate with greenhouses and tropic rainforests, and that smell was now forcing its way into the landing barge.

Some mariners will say that after a long crossing, the smell of land is evident, even 50 miles out.

We obviously were considerably closer, because the anchor chain was rattling down. Rotuma's only wharf, at Oinafa, isn't approachable at night because there are protruding coral heads almost in the channel. That meant I had a few hours to go before I could get my first glimpse of the island which had been described so captivatingly in the logs of just about every ship which had passed by...

"The main island far exceeds in populousness and fertility all that we had seen in this sea...the evidently superior fertility of the island, and the seeming cheerful and friendly disposition of the natives, makes this, in our opinion, the most eligible place for ships coming from the eastward, wanting refreshments, to touch at; and with regard to missionary views...there can hardly be a place where they could settle with greater advantage, as there is food in abundance; and the island, lying remote from others, can never be engaged in wars..."

So wrote William Wilson on the missionary ship *Duff* in 1797.

HMS Pandora had arrived and discovered Rotuma six years earlier. Captain Edwards on Pandora was impressed with the island's fertility, both in soil and population, noting it was "as well or better cultivated and its inhabitants more numerous for its size than any of the islands we have hitherto seen."

As far as the 'friendly disposition of the natives' went, welcomes hadn't quite been perfected.

"They came off in a fleet of canoes, rested on their paddles, and gave the war whoop at stated periods. They were all armed with clubs, and meant to attack us, but the magnitude and novelty of such an object as a man of war, struck them with a mixture of wonder and fear."

George Hamilton, *Pandora's* surgeon, 1791.

The Duiyabaki's greeting party was less dramatic. A parade of headlights began moving through the pre-dawn blackness, and by first light, three dark green PWD trucks and a fleet of motorbikes waited on the wharf as we slid alongside.

Pacific fish such as the *mahimahi*, as any fisherman knows, go through incredible transitions of colour just after being caught. They come out of the water gray, but then seem to put everything they've got into a show-must-go-on splash of colour.

That's what happened alongside the wharf at Oinafa.

My first impression was a monotone of black and grays. The surrounding beaches were white, but monstrous clumps of coal-black lava studded the shoreline. As the light intensified, the sea turned from a dull gray to a brilliant aquamarine, reflecting off the white and gold sands beneath the landing barge. The green of Rotuma exploded across the water.

A missionary who had visited this isolated outpost in 1852, John Williams, had called it the most emerald island in the central Pacific. I could see why.

I only vaguely noticed the scurry of activity as the Duiyabaki prepared to unload 55 tons of cargo: three Caterpillar tractors, drums of fuel and explosives to forge an airstrip.

If anyone doubted that change was coming to Rotuma, their doubts wouldn't last for long.

"I think the airstrip will be an advantage because transport will be easier and things like mail will be here often. When they open the airstrip, it is likely that there will be plenty of jobs for the youths that are roaming around doing nothing now, such as taking tourists to outer islands for sightseeing and so forth, to earn some money rather than staying at home cutting copra.

Another advantage is that people will be westernized in some ways by things they see from foreigners. But things can go the other way around...customs will not be followed by tourists; clothing and ways will change a great deal. The Rotumans are going to pretend to act like Europeans, and that makes older people angry."

Arieta Kaurasi, Form 5, Rotuma High School.

Rotuma's isolation is both curse and salvation. Salvation to the elders who are content with the status quo: nothing changes very fast here, to which the elders say 'whoopee'. Or the equivalent.

Sociologists say that the reason the Rotumans lost the art of building sea-going canoes was because they had no desire to go anywhere else. Their 17 square miles of fertile volcanic soil was all they needed.

But try to talk about the joy and purity of that lonely, reef-bound paradise to an 18-year-old Rotuman, and he or she will talk to you instead about Suva. All Rotumans acknowledge that their island is good, but the lure of higher education, jobs, disco music and new sights is strong.

"...in Rotuma, the children come to Suva to wait for their Fiji Junior Certificate results. Why can they not wait in Rotuma? If they pass, they are promised further education, but those who fail stay on in Suva and try to find jobs. Unfortunately, the parents back the children; they want the children to find jobs in Suva and send money back home. In Rotuma, we have been promised electricity, and when this does eventuate, our children will not need to go to the urban areas to see the bright lights..."

Senator Wilson Inia of Rotuma in the Senate, 1980.

There was a New Zealander named Tom Neale who has a fan club of sorts spread around the world. Tom Neale managed to spend 10 or 12 years living entirely by himself on a little island called Suwarrow in the Cooks, visited once or twice a year by passing yachts. Yachties worship his memory and still tread on his island as if it were a shrine.

Which it is.

They will relate the magic they caught from reading Tom Neale's book, An Island to Oneself. With eyes shining fire, they will speak of the obvious peace Tom discovered by living in a community of one.

I, too, am a Tom Neale worshipper. But I learned a lot in Rotuma. I learned I could not be Tom Neale.

Even with 3000 people and all the pork and dalo I could eat, the claustrophobia began to creep in. No potatoes. Certainly no Roquefort dressing. The flies, and there are many, many of them, began to annoy me.

But Rotuma is full of Tom Neales. The people are so self-sufficient that the two co-operative stores stock practically nothing and nobody worries. Between ships, which until very recently were at least two months apart, the shops run out of basics like rice and 'store bought' cigarettes.

To this, the Rotumans say *fia'ama*. So what?

There are about 4000 Rotumans who are not Tom Neales. That is because they left the island, most of them for good. There are twice as many Rotumans living in the rest of Fiji as there are on Rotuma itself. They are bank clerks, advertising consultants, school teachers, civil servants. Isolation does not charm everyone.

Having insinuated that it is difficult to find camembert cheese, cold beer and Caesar salad on the island, let me hurriedly point out that I have never seen a hungry Rotuman.

Hemingway had a dead-ringer for a book title when he named one A Moveable Feast. I wish I'd thought of it. My first feast began the day I arrived and it never ended. That first day, the Methodists were having their annual conference. They pulled up 10,000 dalo to serve, a *kiu*, a word which in fact means that 10,000 dalo have been pulled up for a feast. A thousand people came. They devoured 45 pigs and 22 cattle, but most of the dalo sat in a stacked line across the horizon. No, they said, none of the dalo would be wasted, because they would take it home to eat. Since they were feasting, they wouldn't have time to go to the gardens and then cook...

In this part of the Pacific, as it is in Samoa and Tonga, the wider girth you have, the better you look. I watched round, fleshy women attacking mounds of pork fat.

From the age of 15, Rotuman girls daily become more beautiful.

Eating is all part of hospitality, and the Rotumans are hospitable to themselves, their neighbors, and to the island's few visitors.

Most families have a pig sty somewhere back in the bush, the animals fenced off by rows of black volcanic stone. For almost any special gathering, a church function, whatever, a pig gets the axe. Add to that a plate of dalo, another of steaming octopus, a fermented coconut sauce called *tahroro*, tinned fish and a variety of sweet puddings called *fekei*, and you have the makings of a reasonable lunch.

Ah, you've noticed the menu included tinned fish, eh? The deep sea all around and people eat fish from a can? Well, that's because the reef area surrounding Rotuma is a thin and shallow band. Beyond it is a raging sea which has had nothing to slow it down or interfere with its progress for hundreds of miles. There are only two or three boats on the island seaworthy enough to go beyond the reef, even in moderate weather. When they do, the outboards consume in one hour what for most is a week's wage. Hence, the scarcity of fish.

This does not mean that Rotumans are frightened of the sea. They go out into the sea at times when neither seaman or sane man would. I discovered this en route to Hatana, an adventure story which will be related a little further on.

I also discovered why Rotumans are not afraid of the sea.

"Rotumans are not afraid of the sea because we all have sons and daughters who have been changed into fish and they look after us. We are strong swimmers and no fish will eat us..."

Vafo'ou Jiare, Motusa.

When the men are not out fishing, which is almost all of the time, they have other diversions. Copra cutting and tending gardens takes up most of the week. Drinking grog (*kava*) takes up the rest. Rotumans do not put quite the same amount of ceremony into 'grog' that mainland Fijians do. The presentation of the *bilo* is a little less formal, but what is lacking in ceremony is made up for in strength.

I learned this almost immediately.

Soon after the sixth or seventh *bilo*, my nose bumped the dirt. When I tried to walk, my head bumped into tree branches. This is a most unusual drink, I decided, bumping from person to person.

A little investigative sleuthing revealed that the yaqona root grown in Rotuma is not much different than anywhere else in Fiji. It's just that Rotumans prefer to mix it strong, from aged and mature plants. Well, so be it. It doesn't take long to get used to strong grog, particularly when there's no pub on the island.

The sessions around the grog bowl, at least initially, included some fairly humorous introductions. "This is the man who will challenge you in grog drinking," my host told a gathering at Tuakoi as he invited me to sit down. They looked at me expectantly. I wasn't sure whether they took him seriously.

I soon found it to be a common sort of banter, a harmless teasing that can go either direction: "this is the man you came all this way to photograph... write that this man has no gardens" (of the man who had almost single-handedly provided that 10,000 dalo, the *kiu*).

There is a certain amount of home-made wine produced on the island. That is not surprising, considering the amount of ripe and fermenting fruit — oranges, pawpaw, pineapple — growing almost everywhere. There are even rumours that it was the missionaries who told them how to make it.

I asked the resident Catholic priest if it was true that Sumi Mission had the reputation for making the most wine.

"Only the best," he said.

Actually, the art of the distillery was greatly enhanced by the arrival of the first Europeans. They mixed up batches of toddy, got drunk, got in fights and killed each other.

Maybe this is the right spot to introduce an irreverent but loving history of the island.

The Portuguese voyager, de Quiros, probably discovered Rotuma in 1606. He called it Tuamaco. Since he didn't call it anything in English, his discovery has been ignored.

HMS Pandora arrived on August 8, 1791, on a voyage to arrest the mutineers of the Bounty. Captain Edwards called it Grenville Island and supposed it to be a new discovery. The King's mariners were always 'discovering' new places, as if they had no culture or civilization before they arrived.

Actually, the Micronesians, Melanesians and Polynesians discovered Rotuma before Captain Edwards did. And there are stories about a Chinese junk, stories that, when you look at Rotuman faces, have a certain amount of credibility.

Anyway, the result was a handsome people with a melting pot full of cultures, a microcosm with similarities to many, but a final being which was only Rotuman. Their language sounds like something half way between Finnish and Tongan, a partly guttural, partly lyrical song broken up by explosions.

Rotuma's legends date back to the Polynesian era, the third migration. One of the legends says that Raho brought two baskets of earth from Samoa and formed the two thick landforms of the island, separated as they are by the narrow isthmus of Motusa.

A Samoan chief, Tokainiua, was close on Raho's heels. The legends say Raho marked the island as his by tying a coconut leaf around a *fesi* tree. Tradition says that Tokainiua landed at Oinafa, discovered Raho's coconut leaf, and tied a dryer one around the same tree. The two argued their claims, with Tokainiua saying he obviously was there first, because his leaf was dryer, while Raho's was still green.

Raho, they say, was so angry he tore up chunks of the island, creating the smaller islands of Hafliua (split-island), Hatana and Uea.

Sometime between 1650 and 1700, the Tongans came, an invading force of 300 or so from Niua Fo'ou, led by Ma'afu, an earlier version of the Ma'afu who would claim half of Fiji a century or so later.

There were other visitors: a few plundering Tikopians, a few canoes blown off course, all of which added to the eventual makeup which would be called Rotuman.

Life was good. Better than a resort. No cannibalism (when some Maori seamen tried to introduce it, the Rotumans were horrified at their lack of manners); little sickness; not much fighting.

Even the kings, the *sau*, were described as fatherly, neither oppressive or cruel.

Then the Europeans came. These *fafisi* were at first thought to be gods, but it didn't take too long to set the record straight. The gods were whalers and run-away sailors, convicts from Van Diemen's Land and Botany Bay, along with other gentlemen of doubt.

The Polynesians had introduced kava; the fafisi showed a similar talent by distilling grog from coconuts, getting drunk and killing each other off. The derelicts that survived recounted how there had been a hundred fafisi one year, twenty the next. Most of them died a violent death.

To which the Rotumans probably replied *liak'sia*. Good riddance. This does not mean that Rotumans were not gracious hosts, even in those days. They tried to make their guests welcome, even offering them their choice of fair maidens. But they didn't like orgies and fighting and, besides, the sailors looked uncouth: they had hairy chests.

Of course, with the arrival of the sailors came a few other things. Like measles, dysentery, influenza and venereal disease. The usual story.

And slavers.

Fortunately, Rotuma was small enough and out of the way enough that slavers rarely called. One that did, the *Velocity*, lost 40 men who swam ashore and stayed hidden until the ship left without them.

When La Coquille arrived in 1824, he described the people as "tall and pleasant, well-built, and full of gaiety, with eyes large and full of fire, noses a little flattened, white teeth, ear lobes pierced with a sweet smelling flower, and almost naked."

Small wonder that the Velocity crew jumped ship.

The early Rotumans were also tattooed. George Hamilton, surgeon aboard HMS Pandora, noted "their bodies were curiously marked with the figures of men, dogs, fishes and birds upon every part of them; so that every man was a moving landscape."

The missionaries came and the Rotumans thought they were just more of the usual roustabouts. Not that the new group was initially less destructive when you think about it: the assault forces hit the beach between 1839 and 1847... the London Missionary Society, the Wesleyans and the Roman Catholics.

They didn't get along, of course, each group trying to gain converts over the other, get rid of the *sau*, join forces. Religious wars began and the sailors saw their chance. No friends of these new arrivals who were trying to put down dancing, grog swilling and womanizing, they took a sudden interest in religion, a keen moral duty to assist in these sectarian disputes. They supplied the villagers with guns and ammunition. What followed became known as the Motusa War of 1871. The Wesleyans won, 12 to 2. Another big clash followed a few years later. Fr. Carde, the resident Catholic priest in Rotuma, sums it up this way:

"We lost."

But that's enough history. Fiji had been ceded to Britain in 1874. Rotuma wasn't included. But when some people started talking about French annexation, Fiji's Governor, Sir Arthur Gordon, dispatched a ship to the island and Rotuma's chiefs were told of the honour and privilege of being counted among the children of the Great Queen.

The seven chiefs were already familiar with some of the children of the Great Queen. But Maraf of Noatau, Tavu Rupeni of Oinafa, Albert of Itutiu, Vasea of Malhaha, Osias of Juju, Aisea Mou of Pepjei and Manaf of Itumuta signed anyway. It is unrecorded who among them stood up and said whoopee.

These days, there are more than 20 churches on Rotuma and the sectarian disputes of old have all but faded away. All of the churches seem relatively prosperous. Sunday is such a day of rest that, except for church, few people emerge from their homes. No fishing, no sports. It is a church-oriented island.

For a year or so, public dances are allowed. Then it is decided that they are bad, that they lead to drinking, fights and babies, and for a year or so, dances are banned.

Rotumans are painfully shy and modest. Courting couples don't even talk or look at each other in public. They might just possibly sit together in the film. Several times a week, each time in a different district, someone hangs a sheet on the wall and hooks the projector up to the generator. The generator drowns out the soundtrack, but it doesn't really matter: the films that reach Rotuma aren't exactly current hits.

My introduction to Rotuma's movies came with something called Slave Girl. It seemed to have been in colour, once. It had a variety of lions, camels, Africans and Arabs and a snake that frothed at the mouth. The movie had a collection of Chicago blacks with red lips and leopard skins, shouting and waving spears.

And it had, and this is the part that hurts, bare breasts.

In the 1940s when this film was made, bare breasts were all right as long as they were on savages.

I wasn't paying too much attention to the movie. In fact, I was concentrating on finding a softer spot in the concrete floor when, all of a sudden, all hell broke loose. There were shrieks, squeals, horrifying screams, people rolling on the mats on the hard cement floor as if a bomb had hit. But it wasn't a bomb.

It was a boob.

"...when tourists come here and wear the type of clothes that do not look respectful to older people, especially the women going around with only a bikini and a bra, Rotumans will get a good shock. We native Rotumans are too modest."

M.S. Fonmanu, Form 5, Malhaha Secondary School.

I asked the entire Fifth Form of Rotuma's only secondary school to write an essay for me. It was to be on the subject 'What the Airstrip will mean to Rotuma'.

There are ten students in that form, and all of them had about the same thing to say: they reflected the ideas they had been hearing at home for the last two years.

Rotumans are frightened of the airstrip. They have a notion that thousands of tourists are going to flock to their little island and devour them. But they'll be safe, not because Rotuma isn't interesting, but because tourists aren't very adventurous. They want golf courses and glass bottom boats and cold drinks and something to do at night.

Before the airstrip, the journey between the island and Viti Levu meant three or four days on a small ship, the deck filled to overflowing with lifeless bodies, the air thick with diesel fumes and the smell of fish curry. Because of infrequent schedules, it meant at least a month away from work or home or children.

Not any more.

Nine of the Form Five students wrote some pretty horrific scenarios. "We may find tourists walking around every road in Rotuma. At the moment, we are free from danger, but in a short period, we may hear of murdering and stealing here." Others were concerned at westernization and loss of culture. But one, bless her, had a nicer prediction for the future. Wrote Ieli Mararue: "Rotuma's way of living can emerge."

(Author's note: the airstrip did open in 1982, serviced by regular flights on Sunflower Airlines, and the planes are filled, not with tourists, but with Rotumans, connected at last to schools, bigger hospitals, jobs. There has been no debilitating surge of hotheaded tourists. Nor, for that matter, is there a hotel for visitors to stay.)

The island is a healthy place to live. It is clean, with little sandy roads meandering along the coastlines. The people are very conscientious about sanitation. But there are too many flies, a product, no doubt, of so much abundant and decaying fruit. Rotuma needs the dung beetle. Dung beetles bury the dung that flies usually lay their eggs in. Which brings me to burying.

Each of Rotuma's 15 villages has a cemetery along the road. They are omnipresent, resembling Japanese gardens of raked white sand with elaborate, sometimes colossal black stones of lava jutting out.

The only cemetery I saw that wasn't elaborate was the one that should be, the graveyard of the kings.

There were 106 *sau* before the system was abolished, and most of them were buried at Sisilo, a small hill overlooking Noa'tau.

Vafo'ou Jiare has spent the better part of his life collecting Rotuma's oral traditions. He says that Sisilo was established after the death of Tafaki, the seventh *sau*. This is what Vafo'ou says happened when the cemetery for the *sau* was chosen:

"Finally the day came for the laying of the foundation, the *halaf*, of the cemetery. Each of the five districts had to bring a healthy, pretty young girl, for custom stated that before kings could be buried, young girls must be ceremonially killed and buried there.

"At the appointed time, the five girls were struck, one at a time, once on the head with a stout club, for their deaths were required to be instantaneous. If one had cried out, she would have been carried away and another girl from the same district sacrificed in her place.

"They were buried, one at each of the four corners in the cemetery, and the remaining one right in the centre, their bodies resembling the five stars of the *'atarou* where the spirits of the kings would go."

Vafo'ou says the burial ground was used well into the 18th Century. Most of the graves can still be seen, marked by huge stone slabs which were somehow carried from the coast. Except for Tafaki's grave, it is no longer known which kings lay under the other stones.

The walk to Sisilo is short and sweet. It is heavily overgrown, the bush resilient underfoot. Alongside some of the stone slabs, cannons lie in the underbrush.

Cannons appear in strange places on the island, as if it had once been a battlefield. But they were apparently collected from various ships in the early 1800s and discarded when the novelty wore off. Or when powder and cannonballs ran short.

Cemeteries usually give me a feeling of well-being. They are friendly, pleasant places. Sisilo was like that.

Hatana, the burial place of Raho, wasn't.

Hatana is a sacred island, not far offshore from Rotuma's mainland. Most Rotumans have never been there, because of a combination of factors which includes superstition as well as the fact that boats can't land on the island and the swim across the surrounding reef is treacherous.

Hatana has two small volcanic stones resembling crouching figures, a king and a queen, and these two stones are circled by a ring of coral. There are a number of coins scattered about the coral, and, strangely, no bird droppings, even though bird droppings adorn every other inch of the island.

There are a number of taboos associated with Hatana. One is that visitors are to adorn the rock figures with a *tefui*, a garland of red and white flowers.

Break the taboos, say the Rotumans, and the seas will rise, marooning the visitors or drowning them in their attempt to reach the mainland.

I wanted to get to Hatana and see the king and queen for my-self. But whenever I approached the subject, I was told that the sea was too rough, that the weather was bad, that it was a day to work in the gardens. Some people flatly told me I should not go there.

Finally, a day came that seemed, to a Rotuman, suitable. It didn't look very suitable to me: the skies were leaden, the sea pounding onto the rocks nearby.

The boat chosen, the *Oholei*, looked perfectly safe for a journey down a quiet stream. It looked absurdly small for the open sea. And the tiny outboard, well, it looked like something a museum might want.

I wondered what would happen if we failed to return that evening. Was there even another boat to look for us? I could im-agine people saying, "oh yes, Fatiaki and that photographer, we haven't seen them for a week." On the windward side of Rotuma, how long would it take for us to wash up on, say, Futuna?

I stopped thinking about it. There were four of us in the punt. We had five gallons of fuel for the little Mariner outboard, four inches of freeboard, and a Rotuman at the helm who was manoeuvering the craft down the sides of the waves, surfing some-times, with obvious skill.

From the bottom of the troughs, Rotuma and Hatana disap-peared altogether.

My camera and lenses were sealed in one of those small black plastic drums that New Zealand exports its kegged beef in. As waves smashed over the bow, I imagined the little keg would be a handy life buoy if worse came to worse.

But it never came to that. Fatiaki Paka manoeuvered the boat as near to the rocks as he could without being carried onto them, and three trainee commandos went over the side.

Coral heads 15 feet below loomed like prehistoric sea monsters. I wanted to go ahead but I kept moving sideways. It seemed to take a long time to get anywhere. Black drum held aloft, the three of us reached the rocky reef simultaneously.

Safety, I thought.

That was when a wave, Raho's wave, picked us up and carried us tumbling over the mussel-sharp stone for 20 yards. The black drum disappeared in the foam. I foolishly tried to hold on to the outcrops as they went rushing past, my legs and arms smashing against them as I went.

It was a nasty wave, but when it departed, the three of us were left standing in the shallows, safe. The drum lay in the sand.

Raho, a stickler for protocol, had obviously noted that we had failed to bring the *tefui*.

Instead, coral cuts on our hands, feet, knees and legs now sprouted crimson petals.

Raho's domain is a kingdom of seabirds. It is like no place I had ever been in my life...so many birds in the air, so many birds and eggs on the ground that it is difficult to find a place to step.

Rotumans like to eat seabirds. They don't get the treat very often, for reasons I now found obvious. One of the commandos began collecting them with a frenzy, most often by simply reaching up and grabbing them out of the air during their slow lift-off.

Later, on what proved to be an easy swim back to the *Oholei,* he would have a cape of birds draped around his neck.

I went to find the king and queen. I hoped that nobody was looking as I knelt down and secretly made a little *faksoro* to the bent and huddling stone figures.

Pardon my trespasses, I said.

A golden gannet overhead turned and nodded.

Tahiti on 'Le Budget'

It had been almost twenty years since I had been in Tahiti and
the re-visitation was prompting a kinetic energy and enthusiasm
which the morning's light drizzle couldn't begin to dampen. Over-
cast skies or not (and it's nice to say they didn't stay that way
long), my reverie continued to climb in tune with the taxi's speed-
ometer on the short run from Tahiti-Faaa airport to Papeete.

My French is poor, but it wouldn't take a linguistics expert to
know the driver was grumbling about the other cars on the road,
even though it was just a few minutes after six in the morning. I
wasn't. I was unashamedly and joyously watching a 2 CV dart in
and out of the line of Peugots, Citroens and Renaults, all pushing
ahead along a tree-lined avenue. There were motorscooters, too,
one of them with a couple of long loaves of bread strapped length-
wise across the back. I hate traffic, but this was *French* traffic, different to what I was used to. Even the sound of a siren was different, that crazy 'heehaw' of the gendarmarie. Exotic shops, waterfront esplanades, I was in a metropolis unlike no other in the Pacific, a sophisticated Christian Dior town in a spectacular oceanic
setting.

Even after twenty years, the *deja vu* was haunting. Yes, I remembered the line of yachts along the harbour and the way the green
hills rolled skyward just beyond the city's fringe. Nothing looked

really bigger or smaller, though it must have grown. Quinn's, a once notorious bar and a veritable pirate's den was, I knew, no longer around. But even from the taxi's window, I could see an array of sidewalk umbrellas and interesting hostelries with 'Hinano' signs stretching down the Boulevard Pomare that would provide adequate retreats.

Air Pacific and Air Caledonie had just established a 'Code-Share' flight from Nadi to Papeete, and I had allowed myself just two days to re-experience this French metropolis before carrying on, a very short time to experience much of anything. Daylight was already well-advanced on Day One. I would have to move like lightning. But the story line was already set: mention Tahiti to anyone and they'll probably say "it's so expensive, isn't it?". So I was looking for ways and means of suggesting it is possible to survive on a budget and still experience the Tahitian lifestyle.

"Did I wish to go to the Hyatt or perhaps the Beachcomber Park Royal?" the driver asked. "Non, Non", I wished to go to the Hotel Pacific at the end of town, the same hotel where I had stayed 20 years earlier. They gave me a room with a view, overlooking harbour, boat dock for the Moorea ferries, and within ear-shot of hearing a bugled reveille from the Navy Yard across the street.

The morning shower had already departed. I headed for the nearest bank, which instantly reaffirmed my conviction that I was going to enjoy my Papeete sojourn. No, it wasn't that Pacific Francs were selling dirt cheap, it was the bank itself. It looked like something Jesse James would hold up, with a solitary teller languishing behind a bench unburdened with bars or security grills, but with lots of wooden posts affixed with brass knobs. The Banque Socredo was not a vinyl tile and stainless steel warehouse and I liked it. One hundred francs turned out to be just about the same as one US dollar, so at least my shopping arithmetic would be comparatively easy.

First on the list, of course, was coffee, and it took a remarkably short time to find one. A real coffee, an espresso in a small cup, black as coal and twice as strong. Power to the people. The girl serving it had a crown of leaves on her head and a saffron coloured blouse that arched low over one shoulder. She had to bend a bit to miss the umbrella. Bras, as I had already noticed in the ten minutes I had been loose on the streets, were not a popular thing here. The espresso was 200 Francs, a kick-starter which would see me through the next couple of hours of wandering.

Shopping was fun. Window-shopping here has the advantage that sophistication is involved and presentation is part of the essence. Not true of most Pacific shopping, where weed killers and hair dyes, socks and axe handles co-mingle on overloaded shelves. In Papeete, bookstalls have magazines on everything — fashion, food, architecture, the arts — and naturally, the 'Filles des Mers du Sud' calendars. Well, you have to buy *something*.

The T-shirt and souvenir shops can be uncreative, but the boutiques and fashion houses try to imitate Paris and they offer apparel which, to untrained eyes, seems quite splendid. Thai silks and strapless gowns and long see-through things, sort of like the dress the totally glamorous Chinese shop assistant was wearing, cause to crank up the old Nikon.

The Chinese shop assistant (there are a lot of Chinese in Papeete, a heritage of French involvement in Indo-China) was also wearing a string of black pearls, which may be one of Tahiti's best-known bargains. Of course a bargain in pearls is not high on a back-packer's list, but cultured black pearls are French Polynesia's biggest export. Black is not only beautiful, but apparently there is more to black than black. Colours, tones and subtle hues make Tahitian pearls the 'loveliest in the world', difficult to counterfeit, and a sought-after commodity. But, says the visitor's bureau, *do* get a certificate of authenticity from the shop, and don't buy pearls from street vendors.

Street vendors, though, come into their own for something else: great and inexpensive star-light dining. As dusk approaches, the parking area next to the ferry dock fills with vans and mobile trailers. Charcoal grills are lit, flashing neon signs connected to car batteries, benches and stools placed. Suddenly, there are about 40 mini-restaurants offering a wondrous variety of culinary delights. I made it past four of them before surrendering to the smells permeating the air. At the Chez Therese, I had a thick, tender char-grilled steak topped with garlic butter, a giant's spread of 'pommes frites' (why is it the French can make french-fries which are crisp and only gently oiled, and just about everybody else gives you a soggy ruin of carbohydrate with enough oil to keep a Land Rover greased for a month) and a delicate display of tomatoes and capsicum for 750 Francs. Remember, that works out to $7.50 US.

And while I was sitting there, watching the passing parade, somebody I knew from Fiji came along, a couple who had just spent 10 days on Moorea in what obviously sounded like upmarket living. And, they noted, they hadn't dined any better than the fare I was getting on the waterfront. Indonesian, Chinese, chez this and chez that, the charcoal grills are definitely a bargain.

The soft light from one of the grills was backlighting a sweet young thing reading the menu next door. And the male half of the Fiji contingent made exactly the same observation I had recorded earlier in the day. "It's positively mind-boggling," he said. "You wouldn't want to start a lingerie shop in Papeete, it would be a waste of time."

Farther down the harbour, Wind Song was lit up in the dark like a Fifth Avenue Christmas tree. Registered in Nassau, this is a sailing craft even I could grow fond of. Wind Song cruises the treacherous shark-filled waters of places like, ah, Cooks Bay in Moorea, and if you have to be at sea, let it be on a giant ship, a wave killer rather than a sailing dory.

One day gone. More early morning shots from my hotel window. The harbour keeps changing moods depending on time of day. Moorea, just 17km distant, beckons. But shops are open until noon on Saturdays, so I will have one last meander, then catch the cat to Moorea at lunchtime.

The local market is large, tidy, and filled with fruits and flowers. Tahitians like their flowers, and not just matronly old spinsters, either. Big burly truck drivers buy flowers. A colourful beginning to a colourful morning. A few blocks away is the Vaima shopping centre, trendy stores with more black pearls and eye-catching *pareus*, both displayed and in use. A pareu is the wrap-around bit of cotton which in other parts of the Pacific is a sulu or a laplap or a lavalava, but which in Papeete takes on new definitions entirely.

Taped to a storefront window: a poster about the 115th Tahiti July Festival, which actually begins in late June. The festival would be fun to see, dancing, sports, even things like traditional tattooing demonstrations. I wouldn't be able to see it, just as I wouldn't be able to see, in my ultra-brief sojourn, so many other things that look intriguing on my map of Tahiti. Waterfalls, caves, the Gauguin Museum, the Point Venus Museum of Discovery, the Marae of Arahurahu, and a million other things on Tahiti Nui and Tahiti Iti. Let alone the other 114 islands.

Well, 113 islands. I nipped over to the boat dock and hopped on the *Aremiti*, one of two fast catamarans that zip over to the neighbouring island in less than half an hour. Big (350 passengers), fast, and with airconditioned salons (most people prefer to sit out on the sundeck), the trip can be chalked up as another bargain...what is 800 Fr. to see Papeete from the sea, and to set foot on Moorea which competes with Bora Bora for the title of Most Beautiful Island in the World. The journey is across the Sea of Moon.

Moorea's boat dock is not really next to anything. The fanciest hotels are on the other side of the island, the leeward side. Cook's Bay has less impressive hotels but more impressive scenery, and it's a quarter way around, on the northeast coast. But the good news is that the busses will take you to Cook's Bay for 200 Fr. I went. I saw spectacular green walls of rock climbing out of the bay and water which was, as advertised, turquoise. I had a hamburger and pomme frites for 750 Fr, a work of art as hamburgers go, delicious. I photographed the hamburger, and the *restaurateur* came up and asked me why I was photographing the hamburger and I said "because, *mon ami*, it is a work of art and I will put it in a travel magazine".

I still had to pay the 750 Fr.

These buses are neat. They're actually trucks with wooden cabins and rows of benches. They, unlike the taxis, are inexpensive. In Papeete, on the Rue du Marechal Foch, trucks leave on a regular basis to go around the west coast; the east coast trucks depart from the Rue Colette near Rue Paul Gauguin. For people on a budget and with a bit of time, a truck tour would be an aesthetically real way to see Tahiti. Tour companies offer full day tours, and the tour companies would stop at interesting places so that people could photograph the museums and waterfalls, so it's a question of priorities.

Saturday night in Papeete. Back to the chargrill cookeries and then across the road for a few Hinanos. Papeete would be a good town to boogie the night away, if only I had the energy. The Tahiti Beachpress, the English-language tourist giveaway, was full of ads of exotic restaurants, exotic evenings. 'Soiree Merveilleuse' said one, with photos of a Polynesian floorshow.

Polynesian floorshows are those things where all the girls wear polished coconut shells, neither traditional or, I'm sure, comfortable. Watching people walk down Boulevard Pomare is almost as much fun. Or having a cup of coffee.

Buzzin' around Raro

There's a lot to be said for a naked lady with long flowing hair, riding gleefully on the back of a shark.

She's obviously a favourite figure in Cook Islands mythology, or she wouldn't be gracing their three dollar note. And then on the other side of that note (and on the one-dollar coin) there's an ancestral god who's obviously quite a myth-maker himself.

But it isn't just Cook Islands currency that is unusual in this land of *Kia Orana*. The Cooks are billed as 'a special place, a special people, a special magic' and the islands nicely fulfill the requirements. There's actually fifteen of them, but most visitors are content with Rarotonga, where more than half of the Cook Islanders themselves live, or the even more exotic Aitutaki.

Rarotonga was visited by *Bounty* mutineer Fletcher Christian in 1789 (Captain Cook sighted other islands in the group further north) but the real discovery came in the 1970s, when an international airport suddenly made it possible for tourism to reach the islands on a grand scale.

So now you've got rental motorbikes buzzing around like mosquitoes, little 90cc clutchless machines zipping along the 32km around-the-island circuit; carved whales and Philippine masks in the shops; mock MGs to tool around the Ara Tapu Road topless; black-pearl stands and waterfront bistros in abundance.

All of which might sound a bit busy, were it not for the fact that Rarotonga is scenically spectacular, the hosts gracious and smiling, and the effort to please way up there, possibly nearing a plus ten.

I reached Raro in August during the week-long Constitution Celebrations, a pretty good time to arrive because something was scheduled every day. If at first I was reluctant to waste valuable sight-seeing time going to see something like a netball tournament, I was quick to discover these were competitions like no other.

Tradition-maintaining showdowns in dancing, fishing, or coconut husking are pretty intense, building on an internal inter-island rivalry which takes even coconut tree-climbing to a higher level. But in sports, the competition is electric.

A woman's netball team from Mauke was facing a team from Mitiaro. In those few pre-game minutes, the on-court taunts came in the form of a backside-waving hula. It must be a hula or I guess, here, a *tamure* — if it wasn't, it would be rude. These are relatively expansive backsides, and the impression is, this is what Mauke thinks of Mitiaro. And vice versa.

The netball bibs are standard enough, but underneath them, the girls are wearing their most outlandish outfits, geared obviously to attract as much attention as possible. Hence the grandmother on the Mitiaro team, not a day under 60, in day-glow pink and purple tights. She was stealing the show on energy alone, a menopause Michael Jordan.

Further down the road, at Vaka Village, the agricultural show was providing ample evidence just how rich Cook Island soil can be, and it was home-base for the fishing contest, too. People went out in their boats after breakfast and came back two hours later, hauling monstrous mahimahi, wahoo and tuna onto the sand in profusion. If I'd caught just *one* of those fish in the last five years, I'd start writing 'The Angler's Guide to the South Pacific.'

It didn't take long to discover that a bus leaves Avarua, the big smoke, clockwise around the island on the hour, counter-clockwise on the half-hour. It doesn't really matter which way you go unless you're in a hurry. Just about everything and every place a visitor would go is somewhere on the coast road.

I say 'just about' because trekkers would instantly disagree. The centre of Rarotonga is high, always green, and impressively jagged, and there is a cross-island track which can be navigated in about four hours. It starts along the Avatiu stream and ends near the (probably still uncompleted) Sheraton site.

Trekking, in fact, is a popular pastime here: there are at least seven other walks that delve into the island's high country, from all sides of Rarotonga, and they meander along streams and climb to peaks which can be 650 metres (2,130 feet) high.

Those pinnacles and peaks are sometimes likened to Tahiti's, a reasonable comparison because there are a lot of other similarities, too...the motorbikes, the turquoise lagoons, the hip-wiggling *tamure*.

Cook Islanders speak a Maori dialect that is easily understood by their Papeete and Moorea counterparts. But 'Raro' has the advantage when it comes to prices: the tourism dollar goes a lot further here. The result is that the cultured black-pearl shops, originally a feature of Papeete shopping, are thriving in Avarua.

Likewise, hotels and restaurants (and there are plenty of them) are booming. Rarotongans know how to look after their guests, and the quality of food and service in many establishments is quite a bit better than some other island countries can offer. Plus the experience is geared to different levels of traveller: bungalows and self-catering cottages for back-packers; swish, no-children-allowed villas with stocked mini-bars for the well-heeled.

I got off to a good start in my chosen spot on the beach when they provided both a complimentary *pareu* and a plunger full of strong, freshly-ground black coffee. Later, the Swiss chef did a rare prime rib of beef that was, well, scrumptious. Creature comforts are nice, like the distractions of a cold Cook's Lager while I scanned the beach for the flower-clad maiden who adorned the cover of the Tourist Authority's brochure.

I didn't see her. I did, though, notice other maidens of undeniable beauty. I made a mental note to come back in April, when the same island rivalry already in evidence for Constitution Week would pit the best *tamure* dancers of all fifteen islands against each other. I also noticed an intriguing fact: take even an average looking sweet young thing and put a crown of leaves on her head (they call it 'le maire' in Tahiti and maybe it's the same thing here) and she becomes instantly exotic. Talk about flower power. It's enough to turn an average sort of chap into Tangaroa, the fellow on the $1 coin. Only coin collectors will recognise this bit of humour for the bravado intended.

In town, and by town I mean Avarua, everything is nicely nearby. Bank, post office, some fine colonial-style buildings with balustrades and balconies. In the bank, I am impressed with the fact that, even though visitors seem to outnumber locals, and the locals have to stand in line while somebody drawls out 'what's this worth in real money', the Rarotongans take it in their stride. If I lived here, I think I'd get mad at the intrusion such a heady tourist trade makes on a small patch of soil. But nobody seems to mind. If people are so gracious here, imagine what the Cook Islanders are like who live on Mangaia or Manihiki. Or Suwarrov, the hero of whom I have written about almost too many times in other sections of this book.

A kayaking friend of mine claimed he didn't care how rough the seas got as long as he could glimpse land. In Avarua, the graceful wooden railings of the Banana Bar are central enough to be viewed as a safe haven from a number of vantage points.

I like walking through Avarua. There's more traffic than I expected, but it's *sane* traffic. The motorbikes buzzing past are a reminder that one of my missions in town is to visit the police post where I need to pay a couple dollars for my driving licence. The licence will enable me to rent one of those little red motorbikes so that I can add yet another buzz to the 90cc drone that envelops the island.

I was glad I did, partly because taxis can be a little hard to find. And partly because, on my very first circumnavigation of the island, I chanced upon a little Japanese girl, limping along the roadside. I stopped. Was she all right? No, she'd hurt her ankle. Did she want a ride back to wherever she was staying? Yes, she did.

No Harley Sportster, this red machine, but it *can* carry two. Our limited conversation revealed the fact that the local supermarket had run out of rice. And she was going to be in Raro for months, a quiet retreat to get away from the world while she studied for an eventual architect's exam back home in Shinjuku.

I dropped her off, dashed a quarter of the way around the island, found the Swiss chef, blurted out the problem, and dashed back with a 10 kg bag of rice.

Months later, back in Suva, I got a little note. Who do I know in the Cook Islands, I thought?

"Very gracious to meet you," it said, "and thank you for all the rice."

According to The Sandpaper (what a wonderful name for a tourist give-away), *everybody* parties on Friday night. Not Saturday, because Sunday in the Cooks starts promptly at midnight and Sunday is a church day. Friday is the national pub day.

I was ready for it.

Sporadic bus service after dark? No fear. Trader Jacks and the Banana Bar lurked on the far horizon. It was time to drink a toast to the *Kia Orana* spirit. I mounted my clutchless charger and whirred into the golden glow as the sun set over Maungaroa.

TAHITI (56) - a burger in Moorea 'to make you famous'; flowers are for everyone... but not everyone can afford black-pearls; 'Le Truck', in reality 'the bus.'

RAROTONGA (63) Netball is serious business, especially when it's an inter-island clash during Constitution Week celebrations. The rest of the time, the island and its centre, Avarua,goes about business quietly.

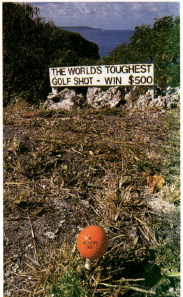

NIUE (75) - The jump into Matapa Chasm is not for the faint-hearted; Coconut crabs, a gourmet's delight; Retrieving the ball is the hard part; Niue's answer to beaches -- sheltered tidal pools.

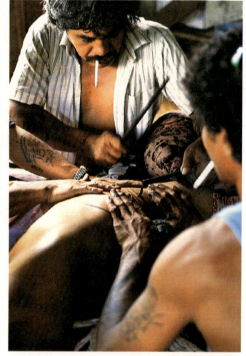

WESTERN SAMOA (81) - The art of the tattoo, 'O le ta tatau', is being revived. Ivory implements like miniature garden rakes quickly but painfully incise the centuries-old design.

WESTERN SAMOA - A village cricket team taunts its opposition (86); other games of 'kirikiti' are less organised. Interior of Upolu (86) is fertile and scarcely populated.

WESTERN SAMOA - A
Savai'i blowhole vents
its fury to the delight of
village youth; roadside
fish sales and Apia flag-
raising ceremony are
six-day-a-week Upolu
(86) rituals; AMERICAN
SAMOA - Tisa behind
the bar (92) in her Pago
Pago retreat.

Niue's Monastic Calm

We were roaring down the road between Alofi and Matapa Chasm at about 30 km per hour. It's a good road, flat and sealed. It's just that people in Niue don't seem to drive hell-for-leather just because they're on pavement.

The car radio was the only noise breaking the tranquility. That, and the hum of the tyres. "Remember, there's no games tomorrow," said the radio announcer. "We've got a busy day ahead of us...the plane is coming in."

Pretty busy, all right. Maybe twenty people getting off the flight, temporarily bolstering Niue's population of 2,000. But then, peace and quiet is what this tiny island country is all about. 'Discover Tranquility' is Niue's tourism slogan, and tranquility is all around us. I like it.

I've just heard another good tourism slogan, too. Des Hipa, the chap driving me to Matapa, is humming along and saying "Niue weather is beautiful one day and perfect the next." And at this very moment, I can't possibly disagree.

For a start, I like what the island looks like. It's a flat table top with cliffs on all sides. Good vegetation and green, and raised up from the sea 40 meters or so. No threat of tidal waves sweeping over anyone here.

I'd heard that beaches were pretty scarce, the sea so deep off the cliff edges that people catch tuna casting from the shore. But who needs beaches when there's glistening rock pools all over, natural amphitheatres of stone filled with sparkling, turquoise water. These wonderful swimming holes dot the coastline, and they're shark and undertow-free. Some take just a bit of getting to, and here the Niue Tourist Authority has poured thin, winding lanes of concrete through the jagged rock to help wayfarers reach the sea. And steps - or ladders - if the way down gets too steep.

Most of these access lanes, about a foot wide, meander through coastal pinnacles of rock which come to a needle point, a defense line of lava shark teeth, jagged and menacing. Paratroopers and hang-glider enthusiasts are unlikely to choose Niue as a training ground.

In fact, only about 700 tourists a year *do* choose Niue as a destination, which adds to the charm. The island can actually cater for about 100 visitors at a time and still leave the lifestyle intact.

"People are hunting for this sort of thing," says Stafford Guest, proprietor of a cliff-top, five-cottage motel — if motel is the word to use on an island with a few hundred cars — called Coral Gardens, and an equally fine restaurant called 'Sails'. "There aren't too many places in the world like it...nobody locks doors, the jail has been closed for years because there wasn't anybody in it, the fishing is fantastic."

On the wall at Sails, there's a huge colour blow-up of a monstrous marlin, hooked and landed from a five-meter 'tinny'. And, earlier in the morning, I'd watched as a veteran fisherman hauled in his aluminium boat onto the wharf with the gantry, staring in amazement at the yellow-fin tuna, a boat-wide wahoo, and other fish dumped in the bottom. He'd been fishing "an hour or two."

This was starting to look like my kind of country, and, as if to emphasize the point, I spotted a feeding turtle just off the shoreline and elegant, long-tailed tropic birds called *tuaki* winging overhead.

Stafford watches the coastline, too, keeping a record on whales. For the first time this year, he spotted narwhals, the ocean's unicorns. He also noted that the humpbacks were getting later each year. Obviously, they're adjusting to the Polynesian life-style.

But something else he'd said caught my attention. Nobody in jail? I hustled down to talk to the Chief of Police, Roly Williams, who confirmed that the jail had indeed been closed down. The key has been hanging in the station closet since 1991. A couple cells are kept swept out, and if somebody guzzles too many Fosters and gets a trifle noisy, well, the lock-up is available. But what a fine thing to say about a country: no prison, no prisoners.

One reason is that everybody knows everybody else. It's hard to get into too much mischief in a community of 2000. Steal a car? Where would you take it? The police jotter is pretty well limited to road mishaps and devious crimes like failing to wear a helmet on a motorbike.

Roly is the most amiable police officer imaginable, with the possible exception of his second-in-command, a most fetching sergeant in a dark blue skirt, who asked dutifully if she was allowed to smile while having her picture taken...and then couldn't restrain from a melting grin. She didn't melt; I did.

And when we nipped out to see this formidable prison, I was subjected to tales of the brutal life for prisoners on Niue: how their families provided the *umu* on Sunday, and how prisoners collected and sold golf balls from the adjoining 9-holes in order to make a little pocket money — and sometimes even got a round in themselves.

The Chief of Police has been in Niue less than six months, seconded from New Zealand. Which is true of a lot of things in Niue. The island uses Kiwi currency, receives Kiwi aid, and lives off the earnings sent back by thousands of people who left Niue for bigger, if not greener, pastures.

Niue's population is decidedly on the decline. Where once there were five primary schools, now there is only one. Not only are there empty houses, there seem to be entire empty villages. The Niue phone book is so thin that, well, remember the days when bar machos used to show their muscles by ripping city phone books in half? Niue's is one that even I could manage.

Alofi's the main town. Clean, enough shops to buy necessities like outboard motors or baby strollers, a blue dress or red wine. Nothing too fancy. A daily bakery, nice market, locally-produced television, paved roads on half the island, and even a mini-brewery.

But there's something else that is truly wonderful, and I didn't see it at first. In fact, I didn't see it because it wasn't there to see. All the power lines and telephone cables are underground. This makes the entire island intrinsically more beautiful, and of course Niuens don't have to frantically hang wires up again after each passing storm.

This island would be the perfect venue for an international bicycle race, a 65 km around-the-island event. I wish I could organize it. Two good hotels to accommodate participants, almost no traffic, flat touring country with super sea views and cooling breezes, and a road paved half-way around, basically free of potholes. Visitors can rent bicycles in Niue, and the ride out to Avaiki cave or Matapa Chasm, two of the best swimming holes, would be downright soothing.

Niue Adventures takes people out diving or fishing and the fishing, as mentioned, seems to be super. Dark shapes and silvery flashes in the sun, even under Alofi's main wharf. Next time I come, I'm bringing a spinning rod, for sure.

I will also take my mountaineering gear, in case I get the urge to reach the beach at Toga. The walk in, precarious enough, ends within sight of a diminutive but pristine sand beach. Within sight, but down a wooden ladder which scales the cliff at an almost vertical angle. I wanted to get down into that sand and crack one of the cold cans of beer I had in my rucksack. And then I started laughing and Des said "what's so funny" and I said "this is one place Father Kevin would never come for beer cans."

"Don't be so sure," said Des.

Father Kevin is the resident Catholic priest in Alofi. The can man. When he isn't in the rectory, he's probably out scouring the island for tin cans. Before he came two years ago, most beer and soft drink cans were chucked out the car window. Not a pretty sight for Niue.

Now, the roadsides are clean and most of the cans are either in village collection bins or crushed into shiny, 10 kg cubes awaiting shipment. Father Kevin got the can crusher as a gift from a New Zealand company and the bins from a regional environmental agency. But the scheme adds "only marginal" dividends to the church: the cans still have to be folded and hand-fed into the crushing machine.

Still, there were supposedly 43,000 beer cans delivered in the last voyage. The score: church - half; roads - few.

The good Father is a bit of a character, a trait fairly common to the stalwarts who stay on this island. (Author's note: Fr. Kevin has since left Niue, a bit too much of a character even by Niuean standards). His Sunday sermon would often end with the message "Go with God, but for God's sake, Go".

He invited me in for a cup of tea, then told the Sister to 'put on some Holy Water'. I must have looked quizzical, because he explained "Well, we boil the hell out of it."

Father Kevin is Australian. I asked him what, if anything, was different about his life here in Niue.

"Time" he said. "Time here drives me crazy. The 9 am mass doesn't get off the ground until half-past ten...there is no concept of keeping a schedule."

That seemed a pretty good description of Niue, where even the whales come late.

Tattoo, the Movable Canvas

It is one of the few cultural traits that the people of America and Europe adopted from Polynesians, an art form designed to enhance beauty, to show stature and adulthood, to signify courage.

It is *O le ta tatau*, the art of the tattoo.

Tattooing was a feature of virtually every Polynesian outpost, and so it was evident among the New Zealand Maoris, among Tahitians and Marquesans, in Tonga and Hawaii. Mummies found in Hawaiian burial caves had intricately incised designs, and an artist on Captain Cook's third voyage to the Pacific, in 1778, tried to recreate the patterns he witnessed on living canvases in the Sandwich Islands.

But traditional tattoos are no longer a part of the Tongan or New Zealand lifestyle. Samoa is one of the few places where the art has survived, a vestige of an ancient Polynesian custom which, if anything, is on the upswing.

A young man sits by a freshwater spring along the road to Faleolo. He has a full-body tattoo. A teenaged girl leaps into the air on the netball court, her legs neatly and permanently decorated with an intricate fish-net 'stocking'. A 12-year-old girl in Savai'i flashes a shy smile along with a newly etched armband, and a waiter at Aggie's shows just enough knee to leave two California ladies open-mouthed in amazement. Oh yes, tattooing is alive and well in Samoa.

Suluape Petelo is one of only seven men in Western Samoa to hold the title *sua*, or master tattooist. He's been practising for about 20 years out of his 39, and he does "about forty or fifty" full-body tattoos a year.

That seemed like quite a few, but Suluape said no, it wasn't. He's a science teacher at Chanel College in Apia, and teaching takes up most of his time. He was using a break between terms to try to complete two jobs already started, and then to nip over to Los Angeles where Samoans in residence are apparently standing in line to have *their* distinguishing marks made.

Could I come to the village tomorrow morning while he worked and photograph the event? A nod of the head. But there were certain rules, he said.

Finding the house was easy. The tapping of the mallet was audible all the way out to the road, the dogs were inquisitive but not aggressive, and the men in the *fale* had apparently been alerted that a visitor was coming.

I was asked to don a *lavalava* before entering the house, to leave my shoes at the door, and politely informed that I wasn't to stretch my legs, rise above the *tufuga* (tattooist), or approach the instruments.

A house where tattooing is taking place becomes almost church-like. There is no frivolity, children are hushed and kept outside. But a radio or tape deck is left on, an audible escape for the person undergoing what is described as the most painful experience in a man's life.

On this particular day, Grant Tina was stretched out on the floor, bathed in sweat, but enduring the tap of the mallet and the incisions of the tools without a murmur. Two men pressed his skin smooth, a tighter pallet for a range of tools which resemble miniature garden rakes. Another man swung a fan back and forth, occasionally breaking the rhythm to pass an ashtray under Suluape's precariously balanced cigarette ashes.

The pigment is made from a burnt nut, *Aleurites Moluccana*, or as is more often the case these days, simple carbon black from a kerosene lamp. The tools are intricately handcrafted from ivory, usually from a boar's tusk, and they are shaped to do particular jobs: the smallest, *aumono*, is used for fine design work; medium ones called *ausoni'aso* and *laulau* create curves and short lines; a long rake with perhaps 40 or 50 fine teeth, the *au tapulu*, quickly incises long, thin lines.

The design itself is so old its origin is unknown. And yet, for as far back as anyone can remember, it has remained unchanged, fixed by tradition. Elements of the design are recognisable: the curving stripe across the back is said to represent a canoe, and other sea motifs are incorporated elsewhere on the body — starfish, the *upega* or fishing net, fishing spears, the *fa'aulutoa*. So too are designs common to the village — the *fale* and even the roof rafters, the *'aso o le fusi*.

While oral traditions do not dictate a *tatau* starting point, some authorities are convinced Polynesian tattooing dates back to the Lapita era, and that the incised decorations of Lapita pottery, from 3000 BC to about 1500 BC, are thought to be the inspiration for body decorations.

A few decades ago, the full body tattoo was reserved for high chiefs, a symbol of their authority. These days, tattoos are for anybody "who can handle the pain". It may take only two days for the particularly macho; it may take two weeks or even longer...the decision is left up to the individual, depending on tolerance level. A recent development is that, where people used to bathe in the sea to cool the almost invariable infections, they can now use antibiotic tablets and antibacterial creams.

Grant was using antibiotics. He said he was also "mentally prepared", meaning that he spent the early hours of morning emotionally psyching himself up to it. "It is a great honour" he said during a mid-morning break which must have been blissful. Ten minutes without being hammered on. "And I am ready for it."

Getting ready for tattooing has a lot to do with family, too. It is the family that sets the price, pays the tattooist. When a high chief is tattooed, the costs can be great, not only to pay the *tufuga* but for the feasts and partying afterwards.

Suluape taps away, the mallet or *sausau* driving the ivory spikes beneath the skin. There is no pre-drawing, no mapping out the design. He looks nonchalant and yet, beneath the blackened rags used to perpetually wipe away blood and ink, clean and symmetrical lines emerge. The result has been created without hesitation, with an artist's decisive strokes.

And an artist that demonstrates his talents, not only to waiting Samoans in California, but to tattooing conventions in Rome, Amsterdam and other parts of Europe and America. Twenty or more Samoans now living on America's West Coast , each with full tattoos, can thank the *Sua* for his visitations.

Women, too, are part of the revival. The *malu* is actually the name for the lines in the hollow of the knee, but that name also refers to the women's tattoo, an upper-thigh to just-below-the-knee pattern that can resemble a fishnet stocking.

As for the wrist-bands and arm-bands that are now almost a fashion, they began in the early 70s, about the time traditional tattooing was re-emerging. Many of those are done 'in town' with an electric needle. I expected Suluape to turn his nose up at the mention of this buzzing modern menace, but he simply shrugged.

"It is less painful" he said. He calls the bands Peace Corps Tattoos because, beginning about 1967 with the arrival of Peace Corps members in large numbers, they were the most sought-after souvenir of Samoa.

A small mark, for some, to identify their sense of belonging. And, for those willing to suffer the full *tatau* or *malu,* a very traditional rendering proudly proclaiming 'I am Samoan.'

Green Hills of Upolu

It was too dark for 100 ASA film, but the colours of Upolu were just softening the edges of the roadside villages, just filtering out the final glows of sunset bouncing over the sea when I noticed a truly remarkable thing: every single village had a row of stern-faced guardians quietly assembling along the highway.

Some were uniformed in clean white shirts and bright lavalavas. Some even carried an authoritarian stick, and most took up their positions at village entrances and bridges, or blocked the small turn-offs leading in.

A conch shell blew. What few people remained out of doors, excluding the guardians, began scampering for cover.

Was this some tropical Transylvania, with villagers in headlong flight to escape the approaching darkness and the impending arrival of some sort of Dracula?

Not at all. It wasn't the Count they feared, it was the curfew. A short curfew called the *sa*, imposed by the village churches so that, for a half-hour or so, families may take their evening prayers without the interruption of noisy visitors, honking cars, cheering sports teams passing in buses.

Between 6:30 and 7, chiefs and titled men ensure that their own village folk are where they belong — at home, in prayer — and that any passing vehicles go quietly in the night.

It's just one of the more obvious displays of an island rich in church and chiefly traditions. Upolu. Western Samoa's main island.

On the flight over, the man sitting next to me was a contractor, on his tenth visit to keep an eye on a project underway. He seemed curious just why I was going, a sort of know-it-all bloke who assured me I'd soon run out of things to do.

What I eventually ran out of, was time. Time to explore and discover an island so impressively beautiful that I would have enjoyed seeing every mile of every road, pot holes and all. There are a few bumps and craters in the roads, all right, and the visiting engineer might have found Apia shopping ("we go to Pago for just about everything") a little on the quiet side.

But what I was seeing was an island delightfully Polynesian and proud of it, with an unspoiled and undeveloped charm which leaves some far-fancier and gilded tourist Meccas for dead.

Apia is not Lahaina. That Hawaiian port has had every building wonderfully restored, renamed 'Ye Olde Whaler's Inn' or something akin to it, a painted facade. The old part of Apia, that section along the waterfront called Tavese, has just as many gingerbread-clad structures and most of them date back to the whaling days, too, but they are bereft of paint.

It would perhaps be nice to paint them, but the point of this tale is that Tavese and the rest of Apia, even the rest of Western Samoa, is *real*. People truly friendly, smiles genuine, a quiet, laid-back place going about its business or lack of it without a trace of apology.

I yearned to have a four wheel drive Jeep and take off for the interior. The rental car people have Suzukis for this purpose, but a friend was insistent that he show me around instead. The result was two days of criss-crossing the main island, bounding over the mist-clad mountain passes past waterfalls, enormous banyan trees, glens filled with tree ferns and all the greenery of a botanist's showcase. The villages by the sea and their *fales* all seemed to be surrounded by raked, white sand, reminiscent of Japanese gardens. Samoans seem to like to have their houses visible, without any encroaching bush.

Everywhere, people gave a wave, a smile at this neck-craning tourist with a camera poking out of the window.

Almost apologetically, my friend Ulafala said that, in addition to the scenic ride, we had a little chore to do.

We needed to pick up a pig destined for his church's 100th anniversary celebration and the pig was at the village just ahead. No problem, though: we were traveling in a pickup truck and, as Fala explained, the pig would probably be already tied up, waiting to travel.

Except that it wasn't tied up. It was the biggest, meanest looking sow I'd seen anywhere, and she was patrolling a patch of turf along the riverbank like she owned it, wrinkled nose in the air, daring anyone to get in her way and spoil her day.

"Er, well, when she comes in to feed, we'll just grab her," somebody said. Half a rugby team stood in readiness. The sow came in, the scrum descended, the mud flew. So did the pig, hightailing it for the dense bush on a not-so-distant hillside as five young men wiped dense black mud — I use the term mud politely — out of their eyes.

"Perhaps you could just take a dozen chickens instead," I suggested, but already, the cleanest youth was emerging from a neighbor's house with a bolt-action .22.

"When tradition fails," Fala noted, "modern technology takes over." Sadly for the pig, she was in church the next morning, another carcass under the awning.

I was invited to that church service, commemorating one hundred years of the Diamond of the Wide Ocean Church in Apia. And at that service, I learned more about tradition, about the significance of the many pigs and mats presented, the meaning of the almost ribald dance that held the audience spellbound, even of the taunting and wolf-like howl of a heckler who, by custom, is allowed to take what he wants from the offering.

The service was on a Monday, but in Western Samoa, ceremonies take precedence over mundane things like work. "Everyone understands, even Government offices," I was told. "It's how things are, here."

'How things are' includes the pall of smoke that lays heavily over the entire island group each Sunday morning. Sunday is *umu* day, when the special meal of the week is put into the earth oven. Most village churches decree that the *umu* will be lit well before day-break, so that cooking is completed before morning church services.

My own personal custom and tradition dictates that I have a beer in the evening, and I would like to think that I found, in

Apia, at least two of the Pacific's better watering holes. One was a seaside retreat almost on the wharf, the barmaids uniformly wearing fetching smiles and wrist tattoos. Polynesians have great eyes, large and limpid and inviting. Every time I looked up, I was trapped into staying longer. And a bit closer to the centre of town, I discovered Don't Drink the Water, a cocktail bar almost unique in its ban on smoking, with what is decidedly the best Margarita in the Pacific. And with a plate of fresh yellow-fin tuna sashimi as an appetizer.

Storms wreak havoc on the seawall and footpaths, so the walk back to the hotel isn't without peril. But that's the only peril. There's no threat of anyone lurking behind you, intent on snatching a wallet. *Fales* are open-sided, blinds casually dropped at night. There are no burglar bars because, apparently, there are no burglars.

But thieves, yes, especially the barmaids who steal your heart.

Airport roads world-wide are rarely scenic delights. Not so, the road from Faleolo International Airport to Apia.

That 30 km stretch of Upolu's Main West Road is a delightful drive, as interesting in scenery as it is in human activity. Each village has a church and each village has a cricket pitch. Cricket, or *kirikiti*, is *the* sport on the island and cricketers use a pure latex ball and a homemade bat — a three-sided affair that looks like a war club — in six-days-a-week competitions that include as many players as the other side can muster.

The Airport Road is flanked with the sea on one side and well-nurtured gardens and rainforest on the other, some of it rising to island peaks more than 1000 metres high. The *fales* are open and painted with intensely bright blues and pinks; kids and horses and pigs are everywhere, and the population seems more than a little bit interested in noting just who's passing by.

This is a road with a constantly changing character: on Sundays, the women all in white and the churches full, it is pious. Afternoons every other day, it is a sports arena. Early mornings, the emphasis is on agriculture and village chores.

It is, in fact, a microcosm of all that is Samoan, a grand introduction to their particular way of life.

Of course, Samoans have a word for their way of life: *Fa'a Samoa.* It is both prideful boast and apology for a lifestyle nobody on the islands would ever think of changing.

Nude Friday

Do you remember John Steinbeck's book Cannery Row? And the weird and wonderful characters that made up that sleepy little coastal town, and how they devised days like 'Sweet Thursday'?

Well, in another cannery town, this one mid-Pacific, an enterprising gal named Tisa has added Nude Friday to Sweet Thursday. And she's making the rounds of the authors, saying that not only Steinbeck but Somerset Maugham is responsible for molding her version of a fantasy she created on a beach in Pago Pago, American Samoa.

"A fantasy modeled on the 1920s and 30s, for other people to live."

Tisa is host and proprietor of Tisa's Barefoot Bar in Pago, and it must be said that this is a bar like no other.

It's a few miles out of town, past the cannery and along a rugged shorefront, nestled on the side of a thickly-wooded and fast-dropping hillside, almost too secluded to see. The sign is too small, the parking non-existent.

Yet, what began in 1989 amidst a fair bit of controversy is now Pago's bright spot. Rosalia Tisa had pulled out of a less-than-perfect marriage in the States, returned home and was looking for a way to survive. She thought a bar on the beach might just be the answer. She was told girls don't run bars, and beaches in Pago are traditionally used for keeping pigs.

She built her bar, anyway.

"It was a hut on the sand with prehistoric furniture, and tiny. But people started coming. The bar grew and so did the number of clientele."

A lot of them were men, because Tisa is a pretty exotic-looking girl. Trim, tall and tan, and muscular, too, because she cuts her own bush trails for nature walks and chops the firewood for her Sunday *umu*. Stories about Tisa got pretty wild, and the wilder the stories became, the more people came.

It was great for business.

The girl with the tattoo of a Tahitian fertility goddess on her ankle ("that's what people are all about, isn't it?") was, in fact, lapping it all up. "I heard some of these stories and I had to laugh, but it doesn't bother me. Nobody's God except God himself and nobody here is going to tell me what I can or can't do."

What she does, is brew home brew, serve octopus in coconut cream, *umu* lobster and pig on Sunday, and ensure her customers are enjoying themselves. "Now, everybody comes, the wives, the girlfriends, nobody is suspicious any more and we have a terrific time." She takes people on nature walks and cave explorations. The neighboring village has been brought into the eco-tourism scheme and, she says, is dedicated to preserving the old ways.

But there are some new ways, too. Like Nude Friday. You can romp on Tisa's beach from 2 am until the first hint of Saturday's gray touches the sky. Then it's off the beach. Her main rule is 'don't let the sun catch you.'

Nude Friday is a fairly recent innovation, and it probably wasn't even a bar feature during the visit of one particular group of patrons. That was when a US Navy ship with a mixed male and female crew chose Tisas for a five-day stay. A rule restricting co-mingling of military personnel, and rumours of a Pago party supposedly resembling the infamous Tail Hook incident brought Tisa to the attention of the Navy Command. She was subpoenaed to appear in Washington. Where she said her guests at the beach bar behaved themselves with the dignity expected of officers and gentlemen.

End of story.

"I enjoy the serenity and I love the people that come here...sailors and fishermen, families and children. We cook on an open fire, we don't have TV in the place because I'm not interested in what the rest of the world is doing. This is how Hollywood writes the script for the South Seas, anyway."

Destination: Port Vila

Four days to spend in Port Vila. Four days of gourmet dining, exotic shopping, downing Pripps or *pastis* in secluded spots with unsecluded views, and wandering around in a big little town that I have grown to like very much.

'Grown to like', because the very first time I came to Vila, it wasn't much fun at all. That was back in the days when Vanuatu was the New Hebrides and the two factions, the British and the French, weren't seeing everything eye to eye.

In fact, I'd been sent over to Port Vila by a newspaper to cover the riots. A pro-French group was organising a little rally, and I was standing around with my old F2 dangling from my neck. It might have even been a new F2 in those days. Two fellows with axe handles politely told me 'no photos' and waved me away.

I went away. And re-emerged, sort of, from the other side of the crowd. The two fellows saw me again. "No photos," they said, and waved me away, a little less tenderness in their expressions.

I am a feature writer, not a war correspondent, I thought. But then I saw the answer: a fire escape going up to the top floor, the fourth floor, of a building right on the main street where the crowd was gathering. If I could get to the top and discreetly aim my camera down...

An elderly Chinese trader was standing next to the fire-escape.

I asked if I could go up to the top. He nodded. It was all so easy. Peering over the top, I had a news-reporter's view of everything I wanted. The crowd. The street. I could even see the little Chinese trader, talking to the two men with the axe handles, pointing to the top of the building.

I came down those stairs four at a time, opening the camera on the way. The two men were climbing up with formidable speed. I held the film out to them, showed them the Nikon was empty.

"OK", I said. "You win. I'm going to the hotel." And I did. I drank red wine and, when the day's events were over, telephoned a picture-less feature back to the newspaper. Port Vila, circa 1977.

In the years that followed, I've been back to Vila a number of times, and I like it more each time.

Each time, I find more to do, so much that I never seem to exhaust the potential. I could go diving, game fishing, gambling or golfing if I wanted to, but to be honest, I don't know a nine iron from a six-card flush. I go to Vila to stock up on good music and good food, beginning at the core of things, Le Stomach.

Port Vila's former administrators left their indelible mark: sidewalk cafes with espresso and croissants, patisseries and restaurants with Chez and Les in front of the names. As for the British, well, there is a refreshing amount of orderliness, wide verandahs and pubs like the Duke of Windsor, leaded windows, dart board and all.

Vila probably rivals Noumea for dining out: there are restaurants everywhere and they all seem to have style. Good Santo beef and fresh seafood are still abundant, but the island's culinary specialty, coconut crabs, now takes a bit of searching.

A couple of years back, coconut crabs were on lots of menus and they used to hang over the edge of an oversized-plate, so enormous were they in size. These days, and after countless cruise ships pulled in and 2000 people debarked each time and headed ashore to dine on one of the creatures, they're getting smaller, if they're on the menu at all. Not surprising, since an adult takes about 50 years before it's big enough to hang over a plate.

I love them, especially the butter-like goo at the end of the tail. But I'm a conservationist, at heart. The guilt of ordering what is probably the last breeding female on the island is too great. I order a Santo steak and try to disregard the smell of garlic emanating from beneath the bright red shell on the table next to mine.

At L'Houstalet, though, just for the experience, I had to try the *civet de rousette*, a marinated flying fox cooked in red wine. Owner Clemente never sits down, dashing in and out of the kitchen, flying from table to table like the bat he's baking. "But you must try the *brochette de crevette flambee*, prawns on a skewer, he tells the folks next to me, and they, in turn, are trying to surreptitiously inspect the flying fox on my plate.

Flying foxes, except when they're on the wing, hang upside down from trees. The people next to me continue to glance at my meal, and I'm suddenly tempted to hang upside down from L'Houstalet's colonial-style curtain rods. But I haven't had quite enough house red to incite the courage, through the house red is surprisingly nice.

The Waterfront Bar is a sort of yacht club and yuppie hangout, but they also hang out a blackboard with some decidedly appetizing seafood and steaks on it.

But the list of eateries is too great...La Terrasse, on the main drag, for great coffee and croissants in the morning; Ma Barkers, named after a robber but the prices aren't robbery; the Rossi et al. In Vila, it is possible to eat well. If I had tried Chez Gilles and Brigitte, or Le Rendez-vous, restaurants that cater to the visiting rich and famous, I probably could have eaten very well indeed. But the symbols in the tourist authority's restaurant guide, the only ones with a triple dollar sign by their name, frightened me off.

So I went and had a bowl of *kava* instead. Vila has a number of kava bars called *nakamals* - they're even marked on some tourist maps.

Some are social gathering places where people go after work, and some the more bush-style *nakamal:* dark, with one or two glowing candles inside.

For the novice, the ones marked on the tourist map may be the best bet. Vila kava isn't too strong, but the Tanna variety is definately not for the faint-hearted.

I was staying at Iririki, the island resort in the harbour facing town, and there's a certain charm in living island-style, all the while being a scant five minutes from the centre of things. The resort's boat nips back and forth perpetually, even in the dead of night. It's impossible to get stranded. And once in town, it's, well, shop 'til you drop all on a single street, a 10-minute jaunt from the Rossi at one end, the Waterfront at the other.

Handicrafts, traditional stuff from the outer islands (everyone has to have their very own penis gourd); French lace or Michoutouchkine creations, the artist who designs clothes with psychic colours to match psychic personalities, it's all there. The market is colourful and fun, and the flowers in the street stalls multi-hued and fresh.

Le Cave du Gourmet, dead-centre on the esplanade, is a joy to wander through: collector's kerosene lamps, wines, chocolates, canned goose pate' and, it goes without saying, truffles.

In France, pigs are trained to unearth truffles, and then the pig-master has to extricate them from the tusker's mouth before it dines on a millionaire's snack. I can extricate them in the cave without any training at all. All I need is *vatu*.

Once I got the hang of the *vatu*, and could work out in my head just what two thousand, three hundred *vatu* was in my home currency, I found shopping easy. I couldn't afford anything.

But some people obviously could.

Including those who were stepping ashore from the Club Med II, the world's largest commercial sailing ship. This five-masted city afloat comes in from Tahiti several times each month, staying for most of the day so that its well-heeled clientele can spend a bit of time on Iririki's beach. It also pulls out just before dark, perhaps ensuring passengers spend their dollars in the ship's own casino, bars and lounge, rather than the gaming lounges or Le Flamingo nightclub ashore.

But I mentioned music earlier on, and by that I mean CDs from the big blue place kitty-corner from the Rossi. For the serious music lover, and by that I mean cello concertos, Pavarotti and that sort of thing, you can forget about ever finding any if you're shopping in Fiji or Tonga or Samoa or anywhere this side of the Ala Moana Centre in Hawaii. Except for the big blue duty free shop in Port Vila. Pavarotti? "We have only these seven choices today." Cello? "Which composer, Sir?"

Easily the best bargain in town is travel on the buses, nine or ten-seater mini vans that circulate continuously through and around the urban area. All for the same modest price. The great thing is they go where you want to be taken.

I want to go to the stadium, you say, or to DJ's kava bar, or to Erakor landing. And off you go, with maybe one or two sidetrips on the way to drop other passengers at their specific destinations. Neat.

One of the popular retreats is Erakor Island Resort, mid-lagoon in the east end of town. They, too, have a complimentary ferry, nice sand beaches, and a homey and friendly ambience that appeals to the locals as well as travelers.

Everywhere, the people of Port Vila seem relaxed, gracious and easy to talk to. English, French, Bislama, it doesn't matter, people will try to communicate and they make an effort to be helpful and friendly. Not so in the purely French places like Tahiti or New Caledonia, where, to speak anything other than French is to leave yourself open to the turned-up-nose syndrome.

Port Vila is a town for all tastes, be it beer and burgers or Beaujolais and lobster in garlic sauce. The truffles are extra.

On the Rim of the World

People talk about the rumble of the volcano. It is not a rumble, unless maybe you're fifty miles away. Standing next to the rim, gazing into the cauldron in the volcano's centre, the regular explosions that emanate three or four times every hour are almost bone crushing, a shock wave of sound and air, unexpected and terrifying.

Unexpected because, at this distance from Yasur's centre, there's no telltale release of steam, no visual hint that another explosion is about to slam against your chest cavity. I stood by the crater for several hours and never, in all that time, was I prepared for the whack in the ribs, the monumental crash that occurred seven or eight times while I gazed spellbound into Yasur's fiery core.

The crater must be half-a-mile across, and the heat at its centre creates cyclonic winds which race in total pandemonium around the bowl-like sides.

Some days, rocks the size of automobiles are hurtled aloft, landing near the rim, in places like the place I'm standing. Today is not one of those days. Certain times of year are said to be more spectacular times for the volcano's display. And evening, of course, is prime time to witness Yasur's creativity: in daylight, the core seems less hot, but as evening and darkness approach, the airborne display of molten magma becomes more visible, the red eruptions of unleashed power earth-trembling.

Yasur is Tanna's most famous tourist attraction, and while Vanuatu has other active volcanoes — I had flown over one on Ambrym just a few days earlier— none are as easy to get to as Yasur. In fact, it's one of the most accessible in the world, not only because there are steps and handrails leading up one side, but because a lot of places in the world simply wouldn't let you hang your toes, so to speak, over the edge. In Canada or the US, Australia or anywhere else with a tourism conscience, there'd be fences a mile back from the crater.

Not here. Not in Vanuatu. If you want to live dangerously, that's your decision.

Or sometimes the decision of the custom land owners, who occasionally despair at seeing outsiders climbing the sides of their sacred volcano, and block the road in.

But not today. Yasur has become the most important thing I've ever witnessed. I simply cannot believe what I'm seeing and feeling. No wonder that people of an earlier era would feel this was the godforce, the source of all creation. I feel that way now, and it's going to take months, years, before any experience replaces it.

On the way back down the steps, now remarkably dark, black steps cut into a black volcanic ash, I think of voicing my emotions to my guide, Chief Tom.

But as usual, when the going gets tough, I do my usual trick of making a joke about it. It's something I do too often, the sweeping away of emotion with a detached little quip to cover up. I say something about coming all this way without remembering to bring a virgin to sacrifice. Chief Tom offers no reply. He no doubt has a sense of humour, but Yasur is not a joke. My being here is not a joke. I am on the rim of creation.

Chief Tom has a car, probably one of a few on the entire island. Tanna is not burdened with traffic. Dodging the ruts and fallen coconuts on the now totally dark road, I see a waving fire brand arcing back and forth in front of the Landcruiser.

What in heaven's name is that? And the answer comes without my really voicing the question. A kava drinker.

Tanna kava is said to be the strongest anywhere. Some botanists think that kava, the pounded (or ground or chewed) root of *Piper methysticum* originated in Vanuatu.

At home in Suva, I sit down to six or seven bowls of 'grog' as a sort of expected Sunday-afternoon session with the extended family. Here, Chief Tom assures me, two bowls would leave me unable to work for three days. Pity, because I'd like to try it, but every hour on this island is precious.

The man working his way down the dark dirt track is not trying to light his way with the burning torch...he has his eyes covered. He is waving the burning stick so that we won't run into him. Tom says most men prefer to slip away into the bush and meditate for a day or two. They don't want to hear any sound, he says, "particularly their wives". "The loudest sound should be a cricket chirping." And they certainly don't want to see any bright lights. Not that that usually happens in Tanna. But I've noticed that even Port Vila's commercial 'nakamals' or kava dens have only one candle burning.

Our return to my modest accommodation at the White Grass Hotel is uneventful. Tom wants to know if I care to see the wild horses tomorrow, or visit the John Frum village, a cargo-cult village whose inhabitants still expect, someday, mana to fall from the sky. But the fuses in my mind are still overloaded with Yasur. It will take a long time for the current to regulate. And besides, I'm supposed to catch a plane tomorrow, bound for Santo.

Santo this trip will be an expedition to photograph known tourist spots for the Tourism Council of the South Pacific. World War II bunkers left behind by the Americans, 'Champagne beach', the blue hole, that sort of thing.

The plane is a Britten Norman Islander, and there is lots of time to think in the long hop from Tanna to Efate and on again from Efate to Santo.

Time to think of a much earlier visit to Santo, back in the days when the Messageries Maritimes line stopped at places like Luganville on Espiritu Santo. I was a passenger on the Nouvelle Caledonie, a ship that took five weeks to get from Sydney to Panama, stopping to load copra on the way...in Santo, in the Marquesas, each stop a three or four-day adventure. Only the French would divide 40 people into three classes on a tiny ship, but I would have to say that even Third Class was exquisite: multi course meals, classes in Pernod drinking, lots of red wine.

One of the other passengers was a dark-haired girl named Maryse, and Maryse was in total agreement that we should grab a bottle of good red, a basket of bread in Luganville, and find our way to the water's edge to drink it.

I don't remember the name of the inlet that was our final destination. Looking at a map now, nothing looks familiar, except that there was a small island across the way with one house on it.

A man paddled over from the house in his wooden dugout canoe. We asked him if there were any sharks in the water. He said no. The crocodiles, he said, kept them away.

Oh, we said. And moved further up the bank.

"Very bad," he said, "these crocodiles. One bit a man right here." And he circled his chest to show the area of impact.

"Almost broke his heart."

Tupakapakanava - The Wave of Fire

Hours before it gets dark, the people living along Nuku'alofa's waterfront and along the beaches of the visible outlying islands begin gathering great long bundles of reeds.

Tonight's the night, a once-a-year torch-lighting ceremony called Tupakapakanava, and it coincides nicely with the annual Heilala Festival.

The kids can't wait.

They're pacing up and down seawalls, six to eight foot bundles dragging from under their arms, before the sun has come anywhere near the horizon. It certainly isn't sunset yet, but the children are staring the orb into the sea with discernible concentration.

Some places have spectacular New Year's celebrations; others make fiery displays in honour of independence days, or create bonfires in memory of chaps trying to blow up parliament buildings.

In Tonga, the most fiery event is a shoulder-to-shoulder collection of burning torches, a wave of fire that spreads down the coast from Nuku'alofa as far as the eye can see.

Rings of fire delineate Pangaimotu and the harbour islands, too, and who knows which vantage point is best.

Along the seafront, the sparkling eyes and white teeth of countless children reflect in the flames. The sparks are like airborne gems, a magical, mystical show.

Traditionally, I thought it would have something to do with guiding lost seamen in from the sea, a huge show of light for whalers or sailors lost from the sight of land. A custom re-enacted each year as a sort of blessing of the fleet. But maybe not.

It's not like that at all, said the people I asked.

"*Tupakapakanava* is just a Tongan way of celebrating."

Marking the Spot

Cemeteries fascinate me.

In English church yards, moss-encrusted bits of stone protrude from well-groomed burial gardens. Angel wings and seraph heads are cut into marble slabs proclaiming that Elizabeth or John are at last resting in peace. Death is a solemn thing, and the only colour seems to be the errant daffodil springing up alongside the stone, a blaze of yellow in a field of gray. The gray and the black iron fence are predominant.

Not so in Polynesia.

In Polynesia, going to ground is done with a blaze of colour: pink ribbons, brightly-hued banners, tapa cloth. Stunningly white coral sand surrounded by inverted bottles, garlands of gaudy flowers both real and surreal. Marking the spot is a celebration of rainbows.

Tonga's cemeteries are that way.

Most recently, en route to one of Nuku'alofa's bigger hotels, I passed an entire family guarding a gravestone. A parent had died, they had just arrived from the United States, and they were going to spend the night in the cemetery in a lonely vigil.

Except it didn't seem very lonely. They were remarkably cheerful about their upcoming adventure, and the brightly-bedecked burial ground seemed hospitable.

The night was warm, no hint of rain, and the six children were posing for a photograph before the light faded.

They were waving and nudging each other.

And I couldn't help remembering the small, hillside graveyard in Neiafu, Vava'u. I hadn't been carrying a camera that day, nothing to record the banner that waved over a brightly decorated tomb on that warm April evening.

It said 'Merry Christmas, Akesa'.

Samson vs. the Whales

"Each time the whale blows, we get closer. One hundred fathom of line is out and we must pull and pull. It is hard to get close, the tail can smash the boat into pieces and land is far.

"The whale has big rib bones. If you are lucky, the spear goes between the ribs, into the heart. If you are lucky, the water presses up all red and the whale blows blood. The whale says 'Oh Mr Cook, you shot my heart'."

The Reverend Samson Cook is sitting cross-legged on a mat in his small church at Lapaha, Tonga's old capital. He has a strong face. It isn't a pure Tongan face: he is a great-great-grandson of Captain Cook, *the* Captain Cook, and the lineage shows. The Cook family is so well known in Ha'apai and Tongatapu that everyone from school children to village elders knows of them as the family that goes after whales. Or did.

Tonga abided with the international ban on whaling when it was announced a few decades back, and a tradition of more than 100 years came to an abrupt end. The Cook family dispersed and the Reverend Samson Cook is one of the last still residing in the Kingdom.

I, for one, am truly glad whaling is at an end. Whales are beautiful creatures, and the ban on whaling is a monumental feat for Greenpeace and all the world agencies that fought to preserve these magnificent giants.

And yet, listening to Samson recount his memories, there is a realisation that, in Tonga at least, the whaling years were man-to-beast duels in which the whale could — and frequently did — win. No ships with pod-finding echo sounders and helicopters, cannons and exploding harpoon heads these, but men rowing out in a frail longboat with a thin iron spear.

Samson isn't a walking encyclopedia. He isn't quite sure of all the children's names, and some of the Cook lineage gets a little hazy. But he is sure that Albert Edward Cook, the fifth grandson of Captain James Cook, was an Englishman who went to New Zealand. Albert Edward was aboard a four-masted schooner when it came to Tonga in 1885. The ship was caught in a gale and wrecked, but all hands were saved. Albert Edward came ashore in Ha'apai.

"He saw Ha'apai and he liked it," said Samson, "and he stayed and married a girl from Ha'apai, her name was I'laise. My grandfather was born in Ha'apai and my father, Ned Cook. Ned Cook had 10 children.

"Albert Cook was a very clever man to catch whales and he knew how to make boats. He taught all the Cooks to catch whales. As the boys grew up, they became smart in whaling at Ha'apai.

"It was only the Cook family. Tongans never fished for whales. Maybe they were frightened, I don't know.

"I left school, I didn't like it. When I was ten, I was already in a whaleboat with my father. But I didn't catch whales until I was about 15. My father said, 'OK mister, here's the harpoon' and he held onto my back. I started with small whales. In Tongan waters, the whales come in June with babies. By October, the water gets too hot and they go. That is the end of the whaling time.

"We would sail around 'Eua and Ha'apai, six boys in a boat, to pull the whale after the harpoon hits.

"When the harpoon hits, the whale dives deep. Very quick and very fast. If the seas are rough, we must drop the sails and mast. Then the fun begins. The whale pulls the boat fast, like a speedboat. The nose of the boat is smashing through the waves and water is flying everywhere.

"The whale may pull for six hours and I cannot see the land: I think I will surely die."

Samson stops talking and gazes, almost in meditation, a dreamlike reverie as he remembers. After three or four minutes of silence, just when I'm wondering whether to cough or poke the interpreter, he begins again.

"When the whale blows, we must pull to get closer. When we are close, we must throw the spear again. This happens many times. The harpoon is near the head, it is made of iron instead of steel so it cannot snap, and it holds the whale. But the harpoon does not kill the whale. The killing spear does that, and it may be thrown many times.

"The whale cries like a cow. Each time the whale blows, we get closer."

A humpback whale, its heart pierced, dies. 'Mr Cook' is victorious. The sharks home in on the carcass, drawn by its final bloody breath. Sharks or no sharks, boatcrew must leap into the water, stitching up the whale's mouth so it doesn't take water, and fixing the whale to the boat. If the whale sinks, all is lost.

Sometimes, the whale sinks anyway, and with 50 tons of dead weight strapped to the side of the boat, it's a question of how fast the line can be cut before boat and crew are pulled to the bottom.

If, in that frenzied Nantucket sleigh ride, the whale fights into darkness, the battle is over and the creature is freed. With the whaleboat being pulled through the seas at frightening speed, the nose up, the spray blinding the helmsman, coral heads flashing below the prow, then the risk is too great.

The whale has won, and the harpoon will work its way out.

Sometimes, in the closeness of battle, the spear poised a mere 20 feet from the whale's back, the creature turns and breaks the boat into splinters. One member of the family, Walter, made a legendary swim for miles to reach 'Atata after a smashing tail left him alone in an empty sea.

When a whale was successfully caught, the first of the season went to His Royal Highness, the King. After that, whales were cut up on the reef at low tide and the meat sold.

Before the whaling ban, Nuku'alofa residents were used to the sweet smell of cooking whale meat wafting through the town between the months of July and October.

Samson says it is a lovely smell which spreads for miles. "Everyone would flock to the beach, crowding on to small boats to reach the reef and buy their share.

"When the King told us we must stop killing whales, we stopped," said the Rev. Samson Cook. "But I was sad."

The Making of a Noble

Stacks of colour photographs are spread out on a desk in the Tonga Visitors Bureau. They depict a September installation of a Noble — a title which, in Tonga, is synonymous with being one of King Arthur's Knights of the Round Table.

The Honourable Luani, senior tourist officer with the bureau and himself a Noble, is attempting to explain the intricacies of nobility to a non-Tongan and it's no easy task. The Round Table is Luani's comparison and gradually, the image is taking shape.

"The knight's circle," the Honourable Luani says, "is the kava ring." He draws a picture, his pen scratching a passageway between the areas for roasted pigs and the area for food baskets.

"The King's bowl of kava will come through here. And here are the seven clans from Vava'u and here seven more from Ha'apai...these are the clans of Havea, Takalaua, Felefisi, Ngata, Vaea, Fokololo-e-Hua."

The pen punches little boxes in the semi-circle, each box representing a Noble, and each separated by a talking chief who is the Noble's spokesman. Both Noble and talking chief have hereditary titles, and both are equally respected — except that only Nobles have the real key to power. Land.

When the description begins to get confusing, Luani goes back to the beginning. There are 33 Nobles, a number which has remained unchanged for generations. The tradition of nobility, he thinks, dates back to the 1700s, to a time when there were civil wars in the Kingdom.

There were chieftains who helped the King and chieftains who didn't. To this very day, the position of a Noble when he sits in the kava ring indicates whether he was born into a clan which helped...or one of the 'enemy' clans.

"The enemies of the King from historic times — and this time his pen pierces the paper like a sword thrust — "sit in this column."

A Noble's title is passed from father to son, sometimes to a sister's son or even a daughter's, but the final decision is up to the King.

To be a Noble is to be a land baron: each Noble has an estate which is bequeathed to him, and everything on the land is his concern. Just who else uses the land, and for what, is up to him: it will require his signature on the form before the Minister of Lands can agree to a farming venture, a hotel, or a villager's simple effort to plant taro.

Nobility carries with it a degree of power shared by few others excluding the King. And the Noble is part of a clan which, by tradition, is in charge of certain things. One clan controls the navy, for instance; another must be consulted about all major ceremonies and rituals.

And so, when it comes to the installation of a Noble, almost everyone from the area gets involved. The photographs on the desk, all from the *Tonga Chronicle,* come into play where Luani's map leaves off.

The photos show the kava ceremony, the *pongipongi*, marking a Noble's induction, and they cannot fail to show the extravagance of the affair. Just like Luani's map, the nobles and talking chiefs sit equally spaced in a huge half-circle on a Vava'u rugby field.

A crowd of about 5000 people, most seated and all, I'm told, respectfully silent, are on hand to witness this spectacle, the *pongipongi* in which His Royal Highness Prince Lavaka Ata Ulukalala became a Noble.

One hundred and sixty large pigs, 60 medium pigs, and about 200 food baskets grace the inner field. For more than two hours, the talking chiefs carry on with an eloquent banter. As hereditary leaders, they have the privilege of casting taunting insults in the direction of other clan leaders. They may refer to events in history, saying "if it wasn't for my son, you wouldn't have escaped the spear" and the spokesman for another clan may answer "yes, how can we forget, but you must remember..."

And so on. The dialogue in the burning sun goes on for hours.

And then it is time. A hush falls on the kava ring.

A small girl, Prince Lavaka Ulukalala's daughter, crosses the field carrying a bowl of kava for His Majesty, King Taufa'ahau Tupou IV. By tradition, the third bowl goes to the Noble-to-be, and with it, the title.

"This is the only time," the Honourable Luani explains, "when a Noble and the King share the kava bowl. It is not the same cup, but the same bowl, and when he drinks that cup, the induction is complete."

Fresh Toddy, Old Lures

They paved the airstrip in Tuvalu. Which is kind of a shame, because it was the only major patch of green in all of Funafuti.

A couple of years ago, somebody would wander out to the airstrip thirty minutes before an aircraft's arrival, crank a hand siren, and magically, the rugby and soccer goals were withdrawn and the pigs and children chased off the field. The intrusion only happened twice a week at the most, and within minutes of the plane's departure, pigs and goal posts were back on the green.

Now, most of the green is gone, but at least there's an airfield. Most Pacific atoll residents aren't so lucky. Atolls have notoriously poor soil and too little land to grow any crops; water is scarce and sometimes totally absent, and because there isn't any trade to speak of, there's little of value to interest shippers.

That means places like Tikopia, the farthest outreach in the Solomons, may wait months for a supply boat with those bare necessities, kerosene and tobacco. Or Tokelau, administered by Western Samoa, but now bereft of the once-subsidised service of a monthly supply ship sailing from Apia, 300 miles distant.

And yet atoll folk seem to thrive on their isolationism. They get cash in the form of bigger country aid donations, and from their migrated and extended families living in Australia and New Zealand. The cash goes on tinned fish and bright blue cans of Fosters beer. When they run out of water, a fairly frequent experience, they crack open a coconut. Or laughingly tell you that you must now drink beer instead.

Tarawa, in what is now Kiribati (it used to be The Gilberts) is hot, a bare degree or two off the Equator, and out of water, despite the gift from New Zealand of a water purifying machine. So they import it. The three hotels convince their guests that bathing in the sea is more fun than a fresh-water shower, anyway.

On my first visit to Tarawa, I blithely strolled down the beach, photographing a reddish sunset and all the people who seemed to be cooling off in the water, practically the whole population of Bairiki. I took their pictures, they sat in the water and waved. It wasn't until the next day that I learned the morning and evening ritual was a necessity based on the lack of land-based toilets.

While Kiribati was hot and the beach on an incoming tide a decidedly untidy place for a stroll, Tuvalu was different. It quickly became my favourite atoll. Sandy little lanes. School children sweeping the school grounds, everyone else keeping their tiny patch of land spotless. One hotel with just seven rooms (no water, here either, but I *like* Fosters) and the Melanesian inhabitants for some reason friendlier than the less outgoing Micronesians further north.

Tuvalu is actually 9 atolls, a modest 26 square kilometres of land area, controlling an impressive 1.3 million square kilometres of sea. Tuvaluans are good sailors. Over the years, they've had to be.

In each little Pacific destination, I make it a point to add to my collection of hand-crafted fish-hooks. Real ones, preferably ancestral in origin.

So when I got to Funafuti and the Vaiaku Lagi Hotel, I began my usual quest. "Well, you might talk to George," someone said. "He lives at the end of the road. Blue house. Take my bicycle."

On those shady lanes, the bicycle gliding along smoothly, I reached a blue house at the end of the road (and the island) in ten or twelve minutes.

An old man with white hair was sitting on the porch. "Are you George?" I asked.

"I am. Come for some toddy, have you?"

Now, I've been a Pacific resident for nearly 30 years, and in all that time, I'd heard about toddy but never tried it. It seemed as good a time as any.

Seconds later, legs crossed, I was drinking a murky white fluid that smelled so strongly of alcohol I was forced to breath out as I drank in. Island style, the one glass was refilled and refilled...me, George, two sons, me, George, etc.

I explained that I now felt decidedly woozy. I wouldn't be able to navigate the bicycle. Worse, I confided, I'd probably be hauled up before the magistrate.

"I wouldn't worry about that if I were you," George said. "I *am* the magistrate."

With a striking pearlshell, coconut fibre and bone fish lure in my pocket (which I wasn't allowed to pay for) I stumbled back to the hotel, dragging the bicycle alongside.

Atoll residents are seemingly in tune to doing without, because they have much to do with. They make jokes of the horrors of the cities, the stories passed down from their extended families in Auckland or Sydney. What a way to live, they quip. "We have the sea, the fish, and the world around us is clean and peaceful." When that world sometimes strikes back with a hurricane or a prolonged drought, it is, apparently, 'something nothing' as I used to hear in the villages.

A few Europeans in the last century have opted for an atoll lifestyle too...the Arthur Grimbles, Robert Dean Frisbies and Tom Neales who have shown they can adapt to a singularly simple and unfettered lifestyle. They'd never heard of Greenhouse effects and sea-level rises, and they wouldn't have been much bothered if they did.

There, but for good wine, Camembert, Pavarotti, medical benefits, and a few other million things, go I.

Tranquil Taveuni

Hot coffee in one hand, Nikon in the other, I climbed to the still-dark sun deck and watched the very first graying of dawn merge with a hint of scarlet on Somosomo Straits as the boat inched forward. A few brave lights on the far shore hinted that people were up and about, coming in to meet the boat.

I was studying that first light for any hint of cloud. I've always said I could set up a tripod in the Gobi Desert or the centre of the Sahara and it would rain, but this approaching Taveuni morning looked totally devoid of cloud.

What I could see, under the deepening pink, was the blue haze of morning cooking-fires marking the villages, and the pillars of smoke above the copra driers.

A plume of dust approached far down the coast, as someone belted along the twisting road to catch up with the ferry.

And rising above everything, a ridge of green on this volcanic island which is a dark spine of rainforest, some of it 900 metres, some of it 1200 metres high. Taveuni is no featureless atoll: people get lost here. This is a bushland supreme, with all the birds and boas that a thick and natural forest is supposed to have, and the principal reason Taveuni, rightfully described as the garden island, is such an attraction to naturalists.

One of them, artist and botanist George Bennett, is about to provide my second cup of coffee, ready or not. George doesn't know I'm coming but that's not unusual: he doesn't have a phone anyway.

Aboard ship, waiting for the maw to open and disgorge my red Suzuki, I had considered a 7am breakfast at the nearby Garden Island Resort. But the light was too good. That hour after sunrise and the hour just before dark are a photographer's delight, and it seemed a waste to lose it, no matter how good eggs and bacon sounded.

Minutes later, pounding down the road through Waiyevo to Soqulu, the dust and pot-holes a constant reminder that this is an untouristed, remote part of Fiji, I was consoled by the faces of Taveuni, people on their way to or from the bread shop, smiles and red *sulus* their common identity.

Women were already washing clothes in the streams. The youngest kids were in the water, too; the older ones in immaculate school uniforms waiting alongside the road for the bus.

I heard that amazing sound of the Australian bush. I'd forgotten about the magpies, black and white sentinels imported here — and nowhere else in Fiji — for some obscure reason by the island's early planters. Of which there were many.

In probably 10 visits to Taveuni, I've never gone past Wairiki mission without stopping to take a picture. It's in such a perfect setting against the hillside, the old cathedral, the hilltop cross. The school is still a little deserted at this hour (it wasn't on the way back, when I discovered a 'meke' rehearsal in full swing on the grounds, another roadside attraction).

George lives in a secluded retreat at the edge of Soqulu Estate. Soqulu was probably the most ambitious scheme for rich retirees ever developed in Fiji, a site with miles of meandering paved roads, seaside villas, tennis courts, that sort of thing. A hiding place for millionaires who tired of urban living.

Except, for the millionaires, it stayed too well hidden. The country club is there, the roads are in perfect condition, and a few exotic looking villas are visible through the trees. But Soqulu didn't ever really happen, and most of Taveuni's residents couldn't give two hoots.

Over a beer one night, one back-packing, hill-climbing adventurer said, "you know, half the visitors who come to Taveuni, not counting divers, are coming under the umbrella of eco-tourism, but of course the ultimate eco-tourism statement is to stay at home.

"By just being here, being in any village anywhere, you are part of the change, your presence is inviting change. I should feel guilty, but I can't... I'm too selfish in wanting to see a part of the world that is so pristine."

George Bennett, too, nurtures that isolation. He'd almost be called a recluse, but his family remind him of his social obligations.

Like making me breakfast.

George seems glad to see me, maybe because I bring a few books and maybe because he gets news of the outside world. He used to be more accessible when he lived in Tonga, and he drew pencil portraits of Kings, Polynesian maidens and dancing girls that were simply unbelievably brilliant. And saleable.

Nowadays, he prefers to draw beetles and palm plants, his two passions, and neither commands a high clientele, although a few dollars trickle in from a European contract to illustrate stamps for the World Wide Fund for Nature.

Personally, I liked the almond-eyed Polynesians better than the *Xixuthrus heros*, even if it is one of the world's biggest beetles, but that's art.

Revitalised with curry, spring water, and the benevolence of seeing a good friend, I bounced back down the road. I've never yet gone all the way around to the island's southern point, to Salialevu, and after half an hour of staunch resolution that *this* time I would, I turned around anyway. I don't mind a bumpy road, but I like it when my bottom makes contact with the seat at least on odd occasions.

When I stopped at Wairiki for the *meke* rehearsal, the dust was already thick enough on the jeep for the school kids to impart a few words of wisdom. Or maybe they were just names.

The road is paved again at Somosomo (the Great Council of Chiefs met there a couple years back, so what do you expect?) and the usual crowd of citizenry were crowding around Kaba's store, a veritable supermarket with bank, rental car agency, fax included.

Civilisation for anyone who really wants it. In one of the shops, I even saw a *girlie* magazine. Ye gods, what's happening to my favourite wilderness?

Well, for a start, it's getting a little bit more developed. At the Matei end on the northeast corner, there are now touristy little bits everywhere, many geared for back-packers, more camp grounds, more little restaurants, some good, some bad.

And lots more accommodation. In fact, development of a modest sort seems to have doubled in the two years since I was here last: mountain bike and kayak rentals, $3 curries. Which, I guess, is all right: Fiji never went out of its way to cater to campers, and Matei has jumped into the ring in a big way. With the airstrip at Matei and twice-daily flights, visitors can be out of a plane and in the water in minutes.

At Beverley Camp Grounds, where a tent site is only $5 per night, about five bubbles of bright canvas lined the beach. The grounds were well-raked, everything extraordinarily green and peaceful.

One of the campers is a med student who's doing a five-week training session at the Waiyevo Hospital. Another is a charter boat skipper from Hawaii who's so impressed with the lack of industrialised tourism around here that he told the folks in Hawaii he'd be "another month or so getting back."

Tomorrow, he says, he's going to pitch his tent at the Lavena Environment Project at road's end, where he's been offered the second floor loft of a tree-house with a roof over his tent top, beach side, for the same price. I'm so old fashioned, I thought tents needed stakes.

Just next door to Beverley's is Aquaventure, run by Alex and Tania, from Britain and New Zealand respectively.

They were waxing enthusiastically about the divers yesterday who leapt out of their boat and swam for an hour with passing

Humpback and Minke whales. Alex was stretched out in his hammock, the sun just going down, and not a mosquito in site. Another hard day at the office.

Of course, diving is Taveuni's big thing, the reason people have been coming to this out-of-the-way spot for years. The pioneers, Ric and Doe Cammick, began Dive Taveuni before Scuba folk had ever even heard of Taveuni.

It is now undeniably one of the world's hot spots, and Rainbow Reef and the Great White Wall are bywords from here to the Caribbean and Red Sea. But this story isn't about diving. The Cammicks have tried for 20 years to get my nose under water and they'll never succeed.

I like the rich sweet smell of rainforests and the funky, fungi aroma of wet mulch. It's easy to see why so many people now come to Taveuni for just that aspect.

The adventurous can hike across the middle of the island, around Lake Tagimoucia, or down the southern coastline between Lavena to Salialevu. They'll encounter birds they've never seen at home, get wet, cross dangerous water umpteen times, plunge through mud and forest so thick a cane knife might as well be a toothpick.

The reed-encircled lake is named for the vivid white and scarlet *Medinilla waterhousei*, the Tagimoucia, which grows only in the high country of Taveuni and a single mountain in Vanua Levu, and nowhere else in the world. It blooms between December and late February.

At 4000 feet, Des Voeux Peak is a single day's workout, a two or three hour walk from the end of an access road someone described as a walk in a leaf-lined tunnel, the branches closing in overhead.

Qeleni Road on the north-east coast is known as a superb area for bird-watching. Orange doves, golden doves and a variety of parrots seem to have picked this area as their permanent habitat and keen bird sleuths probably would be rewarded.

As for that trek along the southern coastline, the three Suva naturalists who tried it are still bemoaning what they thought would be an easy three-day jaunt and turned out to be a hellishly-hard stumble. They encountered not only waterfalls which cascaded down cliffs straight into the sea with little way around them, but more than 50 fast-flowing streams which they crossed at their own peril. They somehow gave the impression they weren't desperate to repeat the exercise.

But SAS Commandos might want to give it a try.

Ten years ago, I would have been part of the party.

These days, I like my comforts a little more regulated. I like Maravu Plantation Resort, one of the island's least budget-conscious venues, where I can expect a garlic prawn or a Caesar salad, heavy on the anchovies please.

Maravu has got 55 acres of carefully nurtured garden and eight comfortable bures, one of them the 'honeymoon bure'. I spent two nights in the honeymoon bure, but I'd forgotten to bring, uh, the other honeymooner.

Pity, because the nights were star-filled and remarkably quiet. Except for the roosters. Compared to Suva's howling dogs, I'll take roosters any day, but they do lack a certain precision in their timing.

Sunrise means nothing to a Taveuni rooster. They precede it by at least three hours, just to make sure. I told Maravu's owner, Angela, that she should organise the first ever Great Taveuni Rooster Roast. She noted it had already been tried.

Nobody goes to Taveuni without seeing Bouma falls, and I wasn't one to miss it, either. But because there was nobody there on a weekday, I chose pictures of the falls I took several years ago.

The waterfall is the same. The kids on the rock are probably in university by now. Lavena Beach further on *did* have someone around, namely a young mother and daughter duo who made splendid models against the sand and sky.

In the evening light on the second day, I drove back and forth along the Matei to Bouma end, looking for things photogenic. That's where I saw the ghost goats of Taveuni which very few people have ever witnessed. I had stopped the car to get a shot of a lone runner, face all aglow in the late afternoon light, pumping down a quiet road with the village in the background.

As he came within camera range, four or five goats jumped out on to the road with him, a couple of them rams with dramatic horns. I got in five shots of this beaming Fijian runner and the goats. A neat series of shots, I thought, the real Taveuni.

Except that when I got the films back, I had my five shots of the jogger, but not a goat in site. And I can't believe I didn't get them in frame. Nor did I dream it... I was raving about the shot to folks at Maravu 20 minutes later, even *before* I had my evening beer. So there you have it. The Ghost goats of Taveuni, a new attraction.

I could hear the bell-like sound of villagers pounding grog, the steel pounder rhythmically hitting the edge every third stroke. This bell, I thought, tolls for me, the lure of Taveuni.

At 5am, French-roast coffee waiting for me when I got up, I made my way down to the wharf, this time to catch Patterson's ferry, the *Yabula*, across the Straits to Buca Bay. For the first hour, my jeep was the solitary vehicle aboard, a lonesome speck of red in the corner. Against a gray sky.

The crossing takes less than two hours, and the rain pelted down, and I was inwardly singing. Because for once, the rain began *after* I left. The gods must've been crazy.

Mud Walking in Vanua Levu

It began raining almost the exact second I stepped from the PWD Landcruiser.

Mud, already thick from a week of heavy rain, rolled over the top of my boots.

Labasa to Savusavu is 56 miles, but I was only concerned with the middle ten of it, the part that, as yet, hadn't been turned into a road. What I was standing in, besides Saivou rain, was a track made from a Caterpillar, and I was gingerly working out the slipperyness factor for the mud.

I had been told to expect mountainously-steep slopes and some heavy breathing. Someone advised me to cut the handle off my toothbrush to cut down on all that weight.

A lot of people have walked this track over the years, a track which will become the Trans-insular Highway. A highway engineer had hinted that things didn't move any too fast here in the far north: budgets ran out, machinery gives up. He said progress on the track had involved some massive earthworks and some 300 ft deep cuts.

An hour after I'd begun walking, I was certain the engineer's anticipated schedule was likely to be delayed. The mud was so thick even the Caterpillars had been idle for weeks. Mudslides had enveloped the clearings, leaving jagged trunks of trees lying about in strangely-sculptural displays.

It was powerful country. And tiring. From the top of every ridge, lungs wheezing and knees aching, I could see only a higher ridge.

There was far too much up and not enough down.

My training is that of a flat-land walker. On this road, resting was walking flat and super-resting was going downhill.

A light aircraft, en route to Savusavu, passed overhead. The people in that plane had no idea what they were missing. Spectacular scenery, an opportunity to revel in the feeling of unity with the earth. Heart attack. Blisters.

Eventually, one of the ridges *was* the top. I could see the curve of Savusavu Bay far below. I started moving a little faster. Running, in fact. Not because I wanted to run, but because my knees couldn't hold me back from going faster. I was fearful of blowing out the radial tread on my boots as I careered around corners.

I wasn't to know that, just because vehicles could travel from the Public Works camp to Savusavu, there would be any. I reached a leveling, a highway being built, wide and graceful. It just didn't happen to have any people or vehicles on it. About six miles from Savusavu, a mechanic named Jim appeared in a white truck, just as my last reserve of energy dropped through a hole in my sock.

Pub, I croaked. Pub it is, said Jim.

Jim began talking of dynamite blasts which were too weak, rocks left after the blasts which were too big, too hard on his machines. But the road would mean development in the high country; already a piggery was being set up, and Seaqaqa would have access to... have a good sleep," he said.

A Stroll Across Viti Levu

In the centre of Viti Levu, the mission grass flashes on the ridge tops, the ripple a singular break in an immovable terrain. The sky is motionless, too; a hawk is the solitary pulse of life.

I catch myself studying my watch, tallying the hours we've been walking since that mug of super-sweet tea at Nagatagata. But it's absurd to think in terms of hours or minutes here, or to count a lull or a rest stop as a delay. Delay in what? There is no real reason for time to exist on this trek across the top of Viti Levu.

My walking partner is an architect, usually concerned with making form and space work together. We are both a little spaced out by the space all around us, standing here in the middle of a ridge between Nagatagata and Nubutautau.

Our walk began on a cool, misty morning in Nadarivatu and we were aiming for the lower reaches of the Sigatoka Valley. For two nights at the Nadarivatu Forestry Rest House, we actually needed a fire: chilly nights cool as Canada.

The pines at first light were wet. An hour later, skirting the edge of the forest, the ferns were beginning to crackle in the sun. It was good walking weather.

Our pre-arranged guide arrived early in the morning from Buyabuya, a fairly large village with a bright new school which somehow escaped the attention of the Government map makers.

Probably the Buyabuya people don't know they don't exist.

We keep a steady pace, dropping from high grasslands into the trees and, way down, we can see Nubutautau.

Nubutautau has earned its place in history as the village where Reverend Baker, the only missionary to be killed in Fiji, was axed by its residents.

Ratu Filimoni Nawawabalavu meets us as we enter Nubutautau, an impressive, soft-spoken leader who is the great-grandson of the chief who did in the good Reverend in the same spot more than 125 years ago.

It's good to take off heavy boots, to delve into a steaming plate of dalo and cassava and to partake of the grog bowl. We spend a couple hours telling stories over the *yaqona*, but none of the stories we can muster are half as amusing as the visual display we're providing for the village.

The architect is wearing a new pair of bright blue canvas shoes he bought just for this hike. We'd already crossed quite a few streams. The new shoes turned his feet an unearthly bright blue, revealed to all when he tossed shoes aside before the first *bilo* of grog arrived. A day in the sun had turned both our faces glowing red. The architect's legs, now prominently displayed under the folds of his sulu, are still white as dead fish.

Children come and gape. It is the first time they've seen anything like it, a *kaivalagi* who is red, white and blue.

After what seems like the hundredth bilo of kava, we collapse on a sleeping mat.

At five in the morning, the first light penetrating a haze from the already-lit cooking fires, we begin winding down to the Sigatoka River. And promptly lose all signs of everybody and everything. It may be difficult to get truly lost with a river to follow, but that doesn't mean the track is easy to find. The track, in fact, bounces back and forth across the river like a ping-pong ball, and we seem to be spending most of the day scanning the opposite bank for some sign of it. Scars carved by cattle and rain spills are misleading.

We're not really lost — we're on the river and our destination is on the river — but it's getting dark and it's getting hard finding a way down stream. Someone has built a lean-to for drying yaqona...a roof over our head, of sorts, and we start making a camp. But before our fire is even sputtering, its owner comes and invites us to his village, Sauvakarua.

Wading the river at night, feet sliding on the muddy bank, my energy level is fading rapidly. By the time we reach the village, I can barely climb the river bank's incline. But of course, it isn't over yet: there's a *sevusevu* to present, grog to be drunk, and because there are now visitors in the village, a *taralala* is hastily organised. A dance.

Which is just what I want to do. Dance after walking all day. After the fifth or sixth side-by-side shuffle, my feet shuffle me into our *bure* and into hiding.

Still Water, White Water

Far below the perspex bubble of the helicopter, a thin cut snakes through the bush.

Ian nudges me and points down. Over the whine of the turbo-powered chopper, I can hear him say 'that's it'.

Incredulous, I try to imagine what it will be like coming down that river in a raft. It looks too narrow, cut too deeply into the rock, a crack in the stone.

Ian gently places the machine down on the river bank next to three rubber rafts. We are at Nabukelevu Village practically at the headwaters of the Navua River, the air-borne guests of Ian Simpson, Pacific Crown Aviation's owner.

Nabukelevu's children have been keeping a vigil on the rafts ever since they were dropped the day before, or more appropriately, delivered, complete with *sevusevu*.

The plan is to ride the rafts about 20 miles (32 km) downstream, with five people in each one. Most of us have never been rafting before, all part of the experiment since Ian is trying to evaluate the river trip for tourist potential. The 15 participants include people with a mixture of interests and athletic prowess.

While Ian does a ferrying-run to bring the rest of the party to the river, the first arrivals start hauling the rafts to the river's edge and securing safety lines.

Ian's wife Tippi suggests we have lunch early, before the rapids. She assures us we'll be working it off a few minutes later. Some people smile at her assurance, others don't.

The weather is perfect. Rain during the night has brought the river level to a 'good workable depth'. Each time, the river varies and can be an entirely different experience. Rocks and boulders that are submerged after heavy rains lie in wait when the water is lower.

We are drifting, occasionally paddling.

Ducks cross our path ahead and there are more ducks in the slow pools bypassed by the current. I'd forgotten there were wild ducks in Fiji. Beautiful.

During lunch, the raft veterans give the rest of us a briefing: how best to hold on, what to do in the white water. The first part is to be the most difficult or the most fun, depending on how you look at it. There are about five main rapids, real tumblers I'm told.

After that, there are miles of river gorge where the water slows and ambles through a corridor with 100-foot high rock walls.

I'm just being told about the really scenic part when the unmistakable sound of wild water is heard up ahead. Two words crack out: get ready.

For me, there is very little getting ready to do. Just hang on for dear life. The raft jumps ahead as if suddenly motorised. It buckles, bends and twists. It drops in swirling holes, grates into the rocks and swings wildly around as the back suddenly becomes the front. Water pours in, but in seconds we're through the first rapids.

In the really fast water, I notice that even experienced paddlers stow the paddle and hang on. Which is just about to happen again. The next two minutes is an impossible ride, incredibly exhilarating. We are racing through a chute of foam and banging into and over rocks, the raft flexing like a bucking bronco.

There's a monstrous rock dead ahead and we're going to smash into it full speed. The raft tips, but not quite over, and the rush of water holds us to the rock, foaming up to our chests. The problem is getting away from it and downstream before the next raft comes through and crashes into us.

Plastic paddles bend as we fend off the rock and suddenly we're under way again, another joy ride.

When the next raft hits the rock, eleven-year-old Steward plummets into the rapids and begins a speedy trip downriver, head barely visible above the churning water. Three others leap in after him and all are swept about a quarter-mile downstream before they safely emerge.

One paddle is broken, two have floated down ahead of us. It is something of an effort to re-group, particularly with one raft on the far side of the river and only one person trying to manoeuvre it across.

One of the rafts has a gaping hole punched through the bottom. It still floats, of course, buoyed up by inflated sides, but it calls for a change in balance. Three in that raft, six in the other two. One of the participants, a fairly robust lady who looks like a sergeant-major, has taken a thump in the chest and is gasping for breath. She's moved to the lead raft with veteran paddlers, for safety.

It is amazing what a beating these rafts can take. Rocks in mid-stream are smooth, but striated rocks along walled banks are worn into knife-like edges.

There's a waterfall, the first of about forty we'll see in the next few hours, in the shade of a riverside grotto. The rafts pull in, rafters comparing bruises and experiences underneath the cold spray.

In an hour, we are slowing into a walled gorge, drifting peacefully through what must be some of the most spectacularly colourful and varied scenery in the country. Rock walls glisten, illuminating crabs, moss, lichens and striations of the earth's crust which aren't quite horizontal.

Their slight misalignment causes a visual illusion, making it seem as if the river is flowing uphill. The rock face would be a geologist's dream, a history of buckling and upheaval as readable as a book.

The water does strange things in the gorge, swirling in whirlpool eddies that catch the raft and hold it stationary.

Tension from the rapids is released by inter-raft water fights. The camera has been unwrapped for the hundredth time, only to be plagued by jets of water from a playful splash of a paddle.

It would have been nice to just drift, but the rafts must reach the rendezvous before dark, or we'll be spending a cold, wet night on the banks.

Paddles continue to dig in, until, just visible at the fork of the river, a creature looms which looks like a praying mantis, bug eye projecting above its two open doors.

The Ghosts of Makogai

Secretly, I think I expected to detect some ghostly presence, a faint aura of watchfulness which would be apparent the moment I stepped ashore. Instead, Makogai was bathed in brilliant sunshine, warm and welcoming in the glow of late afternoon. The nearest buildings, relics and remains of Fiji's leper colony, looked farm-like and uninspiring. On first inspection, they appeared to be as bereft of memorabilia as they did of spirits.

Walls which had witnessed courage, compassion and suffering on a monumental scale now told a different story, the graffiti of camping trips and school holidays: 'Wame wuz hia' and 'Beware the Dreketi gang.'

Makogai is a lush and wooded island in the Lomaiviti Group, visible to the northeast of Levuka. Perhaps ironically, it is still a restricted island to visit, but the signs on the beach warning yachtsmen to stand clear are these days an effort to protect a herd of sheep in quarantine, a clam farm and other Government agriculture projects.

I had come to the island with a Civil Servant vet on the pretext of observing the Barbados Black Bellies (the sheep) and tackling what, on his account, were the biggest, most awesome fighting trevally to be found off any wharf, anywhere. The sheep were healthy, the fish far too strong for my 12 lb. line. But what I really came for was far too apparent to hide: a curiosity, a fascination with Makogai, the leper colony, and with its ghostly remains.

I'd read Sister Mary Stella's book on Makogai years earlier, and so my anticipated haunting simply proved I hadn't really done my homework. 'Makogai - Image of Hope' presents a far brighter insight than that. What's more, it's difficult to relate to the despair of a leprosarium — especially when its doors closed more than 25 years ago — when sunlight is dancing on the surrounding hills and reflecting back off a turquoise bay.

The first patients reached the island in 1911. They were described at the time as a "barely recognizable human cargo of decay and misery", outcasts which society regarded with disgust. They would have been frightened: leprosy was still considered incurable and most must have known they were going to the island to die. How vastly different it would have been in 1948, when sulphone drugs began working miracle cures, and in 1969, when isolationism ended and fewer than 100 patients with Hansen's Disease were transferred to Suva.

In between, for 58 years, Makogai had been both haven and hell, a home for some, a prison for others. New arrivals — and over the years they numbered more than 4000 — were met by scores of friendly people whose spirit and enthusiasm for life was catching.

The colony was spotlessly clean and tidy. And big. Makogai's villages included not only Fijians but Samoans, Tongans, Cook Islanders, Gilbertese, Europeans. There were villages in each cove, separated by race on the assumption that patients would be happier in their own ethnic groups and would lead a more normal village life.

"Makogai was a good place" said a veteran of 23 years. "All the races were happy together...always ready to help those who were in worse shape than themselves. They were like brothers and sisters; it was not the same outside."

Admittedly, the earliest years would have been pretty grim. Sister Stella wrote: "Some of the advanced cases...were human beings alive in dead bodies. Many during the last months of their lives had absolutely not the smallest sound area of skin on their bodies - face, mouth, nose - all were ulcerated and only with the greatest difficulty could they swallow a few drops of liquid. The odour was almost unbearable, and even their fellow patients would refuse to approach them. Caring for them was the special task of the Sisters. A visitor told a Sister 'I wouldn't do this for a million dollars'. The Sister quietly replied, 'Neither would I.'"

When Makogai was being built, Roman Catholic sisters were selected as 'the best trained leper nurses available' — and at the same time, warned by the Governor that he was seeking nurses, not nuns. Mother Mary Agnes, in charge of the Catholic Order, was said to have exerted a kindly tyranny over the island.

It was almost inevitable that some of the island's staff would come down with the disease. One of them was Sister Filomena who, after 14 years of service, quietly took leave of the Sisters and moved in with the patients.

Initial treatment was ineffective and painful. As each new drug was tested, the patients' hopes revived. Perhaps this would be the one. When it finally came, in 1948, the change it made to the patients' outlooks and hopes was electric. Within a week of treatment, sores dried up and the medical superintendent wrote that "the 43 patients somewhat tamely described as 'much improved' would, if I had expressed my feelings more freely, have been described as astoundingly improved."

In the years to come, there would be other changes. The quality of life was improving, with a picture theatre, arts and craft school and a technical school on the island. They had Shakespearean plays and a band. The archaic laws isolating people on the island would be changed. So would the name of the disease.

By 1969, when Makogai officially closed as a leprosarium, the only people to remain on the island were the 1241 souls buried on the hill. It remained deserted for ten years, enough time for vandals and holiday-makers to put their names on walls which the patients had kept so painstakingly clean.

Except for the cemetery, outward signs of the island's history are few. Aerial photographs of Makogai taken 35 years ago show scores of buildings which no longer exist. Those that do are vacant shells.

There are enough families required for the 'ag' station to necessitate a clinic, schools, trucks and roads. When the sheep are relocated and the clams seeded into marine reserves, perhaps Makogai will become deserted again.

Come what may, I won't have ghost-busting in mind if I ever get back to the island. Just revenge on the giant trevally that stole my three best lures.

VANUATU - Port Villa kids are pretty sophisticated (95) but many Tanna children (101) live in a time warp. Pentecost Islanders were the world's first bunjee jumpers.

TONGA - Polynesian ancestry is appealing and evident everywhere in the Kingdom... but Tongatapu's Wave of Fire - Tupakapakanava- (106) is a celebration with unclear origins.

TONGA - Great sea battles with whales in Ha'apai are now a mere memory for the Rev. Samson Cook, a descendant of Capt. James Cook (110). Bullock wagons, the ancient craft of tapa-making and a unique style of grave decoration (108) are part of Tonga's appeal.

TUVALU (117) - Children with few diversions play a game known Pacific-wide as they form hand symbols for stone, scissors, paper. Atoll living is congested on Funafuti, but outer atolls have near dream-like quality of lifestyle. Until a storm comes, anyway...

FIJI - Hospitable and seemingly ever-smiling, the children of Fiji are a photographer's delight. Those at top live near Rakiraki; the sand-faced quartet and the boy by the waterfall are from Laucala Island and Taveuni (121) respectively.

FIJI - A 'bilibili' trip through Viti Levu's Sovi Gorge is good fun, sometimes high adventure; Savusavu Bay (130) and area school-children; Hibiscus Highway in Vanua Levu is planter's country, their copra-driers telltale evidence of their trade.

FIJI - Village visits (and the inevitable *sevusevu* ceremony) are one of the joys of Fiji travel. Fijian *mekes* like this rehearsal in Taveuni (121) are another. Everywhere a visitor goes in the country, the welcome is sincere. High-country hosts (155) in Namosi and other interior outposts proffer their charm.

FIJI - Secluded
sea-scape at
Vatulele; Levuka's
(158) seafront,
public school and
Cawaci mission;
'the hill' on
Makogai (139).

Cowboy Country

Larry McMurtry would love it. It looks like cowboy country. It's the spittin' image of a Lonesome Dove sort of place, and just at the moment, a mess of hat-waving cow-punchers are pushing a couple hundred head of cattle across the river which divides this 17,000-acre ranch.

Steers are bellowing, the dust settling on both sides of the river as the sun etches the sides of mesa-like promontories, purple in this rock-strewn prairie.

Looking up into the mountains, it's wide open cattle land as far as the eye can see. Look on the other side, though, and it's the sea you see. What's more, these cowpokes are singing a *taivoro* instead of whoopy ti yi yo, and the nearest Indian is a cane sirdar named Shiu instead of a scalp-hunting Sioux. There ain't a rattlesnake in sight.

I guess you've guessed it by now. This chunk of wild west isn't in Cheyanne or Fort Laramie, it's in Fiji. But you could still film a Marlborough ad here.

Wild horses are broken, cattle branded, and 6000 head of range beef and a couple of hundred horses periodically rounded up inside a 48-mile fence line which takes five boundary riders to check.

The Yaqara Pastoral Company stretches for miles between Rakiraki and Tavua in Viti Levu's dry north. Dusty cattle drives come as a shock to folks expecting coconuts instead of cowboys.

In early times, it wasn't the Daltons who shot it out with the posse, it was Government Troops against the rebel Hill Tribes. A Major Fitzgerald ordered his troops to attack the stronghold of Korowaiwai in 1873, and their over-keen Fijian auxiliary troops massacred 157 villagers before the officers could restrain them. Riled up, the auxiliaries were a little bit worse than putting Jesse James in charge of the mail train.

But then, this was kind of savage country. Just down the road, there's still a marker on the Tavua tombstone of Udre Udre, a chieftain who so loved his fellow man that he ate a thousand of them. But anyway...

Korowaiwai sat on a spur-top ridge practically in the middle of what is now Yaqara. After the massacre, the rest of the area's inhabitants fled into the interior.

A planter named Thomas came along and bought the emptied land, registering 1480 acres as grazing land in 1884, named it Qeledradra — red soil. He supposedly bought 'that area there' pointing from mountain top to mountain top. One of those tops is the formidable haunt of the Fijian ancestral god Degei and the beginning of the Nakauvadra Range.

The Thomas family sold the land to the Colonial Sugar Refining Company. In 1973, the Fiji Government decided to foster a beef industry and took over the reins to 10,000 acres. They started with Herefords, but with that dry Yaqara heat, they needed something like a Texas longhorn. What they settled for was a breed of Santa Gertrudis mixed with a little Brahmin, a critter that could tolerate the red soil when the sun turned it into something resembling a Navajo pot.

Of course, these chaps don't wear chaps and they call a round-up a muster and a corral a sale yard. But they ride just as well as the Cimmaron Kid, and they can chase an errant steer back into the herd before you can say 'get along little doggie'.

The annual muster ends with a sale of about 1200 head of cattle, some as breeding stock, some bound for the abattoir. Yaqara beef is a pretty prized item.

It's prized by rustlers, too. A few years back, it was just too easy for some sneakin' sidewinder to mosey in with his 'ute' and hit the trail with a steer or two tossed in the back. Fact is, they used to lose up to 400 head a year that way.

So they put boundary riders in all the remote corners, built them a house, and told them to have a little check around, night and day. I saw one of them, a big dude on a strong stallion. If the other boundary riders look like he does, I guess rustlin' has just about stopped.

The big boss is Don Makim, an outback Queenslander who, in five or six years, watched Yaqara turn a profit. He says he's a maize man, an agriculturalist more than a cattleman, but in a place like Yaqara, you become the jack of all trades.

He motioned me toward his bronc, a Toyota Hi Lux with all four hooves powered. We hightailed it through some amazing country, crossed rivers with water up to the saddle blanket, and meandered out to the back country.

Fifteen years ago or so, somebody decided to start a mango orchard, growing a new hybrid fruit that had almost no strings and a small stone. The orchard covers the rise next to Yaqara's entrance, an unexpected landmark.

Except that, where we were down by the river, there were miles and miles of mango trees, thick as bees on honeycomb. With a quick little slice, a deft bit of grafting, the export variety of mango was growing out of the native mango tree, happy as can be.

Makim was pointing his red beard skyward at the grafting patterns of the mango branches above him. He was saying something about some Asian countries making more money from mangoes than Fiji makes from sugar. About 20 times over.

Well, I guess some cowboys would sell their saddles before they became a durn mango farmer. But it sure is something to mull over.

The sun was setting and the boys were bringing in some strays from up Coboni way. It was time to be gettin' back to the corral.

The Gates of Heaven

Getting into Namosi and the jagged shark-toothed area that Rupert Brooke called the Gateway to Hell calls for a little bit of extra push. It's definitely four-wheel-drive country.

But I totally disagree with Rupert. Given Suva's horn-blaring motorists and general disquieting big-city manner, I find the encircling Namosi peaks, the peace and solemnity of an area devoid of traffic, the soothing mountain streams and welcoming villages a Gateway to Heaven.

There used to be a hand-painted sign near Navuniivi village which read 'Great welcome to you all who come to visit our poorest country Namosi North.' Not many people *do* visit, though...it's a good hour's journey off the highway if you go the *steep* way, turning off the Queen's road at Nabukavesi west of Suva, or two hours on the flatter road which follows the Waidina River, branching off the Monasavu Road to Nabukaluka and meandering riverside underneath the nobbly Korobasabasaga Range.

Namosi's peaks, though often mist-shrouded, are visible from Suva on a nice day. For me, they beckon with the force a monastery would have to a contemplative monk: I am nearly overcome with the joy of mountain serenity. I am totally happy to spend the day without saying a word. A barking pigeon, a breeze ruffling the tree ferns, no other sound at all. I stop the jeep frequently just to experience the numbing solemnity.

But, in this trip over the ridge, I won't be able to escape talking. There's someone by the muddy road, thumbing a lift. Sometimes there are groups of six or seven people, all desperately assuming they'll fit in my tiny Suzuki, and I can rightfully pass them by. But not this time. There's only one.

His name is Joe, he lives in Narukunabua Village, and he got up at 4 in the morning to get down the mountain and into Navua to sell some kava. He's heading back home with the proceeds, not bad time considering it's only 9 am. Joe originally studied to be a Catholic priest, but married instead, settled along the banks of the Waidina, and raised four kids. They live the sort of spartan existence most people do up in this high country, food from the farm and the river, with cash crops like dalo filling their need for kerosene, tobacco, school fees.

Driving over the top, four wheels churning against inclines so steep I felt a priestly-influence might be handy, the polite conversation finally ended and I could resume my studies of ant ferns, hawks, cascading waterfalls dropping out of distant cliffs.

Joe insisted I have tea at Narukunabua. His delightfully cordial wife was apologetic. They only had lemon-grass tea, the lemon grass growing alongside the house. Lemon grass tea just happens to be one of the nicest warm drinks imaginable. The kids were obediently silent, but watching: not too many *kaivalagis* wander in to Narukunabua.

When I took my leave, I headed for the bridge which crosses the river a few miles upriver. There's a delightful pool, surrounded by monstrous rock cliffs, a great spot for a cooling dip and a little soothing meditation. The air smells so different up here. There's bamboos all along the river.

There have been times in recent years when I've settled in the midst of a Namosi pool, far from the nearest village, with a cold beer in hand, the water gently lapping up to my middle, and a chicken barbequeing on the bank. This of course is not the monastic way, although a few beers under a green mantle of living ferns and vines can be extremely contemplative.

And, twice, I've flown over the Namosi Gorge in a helicopter. Parrots and peregrines look up at the intrusion. The pilot likened it to some part of China, and as the perspex bubble darted over a vertical wall that dropped a couple of hundred feet, my stomach rose up in my throat. Namosi is more than a heart-felt experience.

Sundays, people are on the road, hymn books in hand, immaculately dressed, as they march to their particular church. Just about each village has one. Weekdays, the villages are quiet: kids are in school and the men are in the garden which, as often as not, seems to be a precarious patch cut away halfway up a mountainside. Dalo with a view.

Saturday is a good day to visit Namosi. Everybody resting in the village, the pleasant bell-like sound of somebody pounding grog. These days, I take dried peas for Joe's kids (their absolute *favourite*) and old National Geographics. Namosi folk, young and old, enjoy seeing what the rest of the world looks like.

"It looks like China," I told them, remembering the helicopter pilot. "It looks like heaven."

Another Time, Another Pace

It is Maugham, maybe. All those amazing old colonial homes on the hillsides, their top-hinged window shutters held open with sticks, their interiors filled with polished brass and overstuffed chairs. But it is John Steinbeck, too, a cannery row with red-painted iron sheds and other nearly-discarded remnants of history, a community kept alive by fish packing.

In Levuka, the sea is provider and partitioner, a wall tidily pushing the town into the mountains. "It'll rain tomorrow," says a Levuka veteran "because, look, you can see six islands out there, and the only time that happens, seeing them so clearly, is when there's a ridge of low pressure." People here live by the sea, know the sea, literally breathe the iodine scent of the sea. When they're not breathing the cannery.

After a day spent trekking around Levuka town, I make a joke about signing up a mountaineering team and establishing a base camp halfway up Mission Hill. Everywhere you go in this place, there are steps to climb, 200 here, 190 there, a mere 50 or 60 to get there. When Levuka was Fiji's capital, the flat land along the seawall was used up fast, and folks began climbing the hills. The graying concrete stairs are a legacy of their upward mobility.

This town is not only rich in history, it *looks* like history. Levuka is so comfortable with its past that it doesn't need any Lahaina glitz, no 'Ye Olde Shoppe' stuff to portray its character. Those false-fronts on Beach Street shops, the colonial-era gingerbread bolstering homes, offices and schools are real. This is a town from another time, another pace.

And speaking of time, a church bell tolls the hours, every hour, every half-hour. *Bong* times 180. Crowing roosters do, too, but they're less exact.

This is the place where Seru Cakobau proclaimed himself Cakobau Rex, and the drums rolled as he named his government. A speedily-formed Ku Klux Klan tried to convince him otherwise, part of a whole barrage of beachcombers who wanted in on the act. It was where the same Cakobau, citing "the white stalkers on the beach, the cormorants (who) will open their maws and swallow us" ceded Fiji to Britain on October 10, 1874. The Cession Stone is one of many markers along the waterfront.

John Brown Williams is buried on the edge of town, his gravestone recently whitewashed to the point where the name is almost illegible. Williams distinguished himself as the US Trade Commissioner turned Consul, who so aggravated Cakobau with exaggerated claims for compensation that he virtually forced Fiji to become a British colony.

Ah, what a town. Levuka in the 1870s was booming, a hodgepodge 3000 Europeans, some derelicts and debtors, runaway sailors and whalers, some bona fide planters drawn to the islands by the collapse of America's cotton industry following the Civil War.

Ship captains, it is said, could find their way into port by following the line of floating rum bottles. Well, maybe. In 1872, barrister Robert Philp described Levuka's residents as spending "a great part of the day and night tippling in the public house bars, and of the row of houses which make up Levuka, fully half are hotels and public houses."

What a jolly good party.

The Fiji Times commented about the same time on the "constant report of firearms, night and day" and noted many of the citizenry were "fit inmates for a lockup". The Fiji Times was the first newspaper and Levuka, as the first capital, was of course a town of firsts. The public school, Masonic lodge, bank, Royal Hotel were all the first in the country. I'm not sure about the bank, but the rest are all there, the school still filled with hundreds of kids, the hotel filled with perhaps a half-dozen souls who either relish the archaic ambience or the turn-of-the-century prices.

Some of those damnable steps are probably firsts, too.

But, blocked by vertical slopes on one side and the sea on the other, Levuka was a town with nowhere to grow. In 1881, the capital was shifted to Suva. Never mind that Suva was described as a 'pestiferous swamp'... it had space and a harbour.

Not everybody left, but a lot did. Those that stayed fit an apt description written by Somerset Maugham: "Sometimes a man hits upon a place to which he mysteriously feels that he belongs."

A lot of people feel that about Levuka, right now, today.

Some of them have lived here all their life, or most of it, people like Emma Dora Patterson, 93. Some are new arrivals who have been clobbered with an almost missionary zeal to be a part of this un-cosmopolitan relic of the past, self-proclaimed guardians of the realm.

Dora was born a planter's daughter in Vanua Levu, marrying and moving to Levuka when she was 22. She lives on a hilltop, up 176 steps, in the same house where she raised her four sons. She still climbs those steps for exercise and thumbs through a stack of photographs to show visitors her expanded family. The family is now in New Zealand and Australia and husband Reg died a long time back, but 'Aunty Dora' stays fit on a prescription of visitors and memories. She remembers the horse track on the hilltop just above her house: Reg was one of many who imported the best racing stock that Australia had to offer, and race day on the hill must have been quite an event.

She remembers a Levuka during World War II, a grand time when New Zealand and American army officers were billeted in the town and there was a dance almost every night.

Even as a young girl, when she still lived in Savusavu, she schooled in Levuka, sailing back and forth on the cutter 'Emma', dodging hurricanes and, when there was no wind at all or too much of it, spending the night at Namena in a cave. The cave, she said, was good fun.

She's been invited to (and attended) the Queen's garden party at Buckingham Palace, chatted with Elizabeth Rex once in Fiji and again in New Zealand ("bless her heart, I didn't even know she was *in* New Zealand") and visited with Prince Charles twice. She agreed that it wouldn't hurt the Queen to smile more ("her husband Philip had to nudge her in public and she smiled straight away, but I think the poor girl is just shy. But isn't Prince Charles a lovely chap, so likeable?")

Skirmishes with Royalty.

Royalty in Levuka usually has something to do with staying in the Ashleys' Royal Hotel, dark as a cave inside, the brass shining, early pictures of the town on its walls. It's often hard to get a room there, not because the Royal is filled up, but because guests are just too upsetting to the lifestyle. The Royal is a hotel that exists unto its own and guests can be an inconvenience.

An equal number of steps up the hill, next door to Dora, in fact, is the Brook home. Mike and Jennifer Brook run a tour operation, taking people out to see the old church at St. John's College, Cawaci; the Bishop's Tomb on a hill overlooking the church, and anywhere else visitors want to go. Mike is involved with everything connected to heritage: he's one of those people who isn't content to sit back and watch the town dwindle away, even if the town wants to. It's sort of like helping a little old lady across the street when she doesn't want to go. Their current project: fundraising to restore the Bishop's Tomb, which at the moment has most of its windows broken out, the door left open, the paint peeling.

But, like Maugham said, some people feel *this* is the place, whether they were born here or wandered in.

Wandering in is what most Levuka visitors do. After all, the town is only a 12-minute Air Fiji flight from Nausori, not exactly the end of the world. They've heard the town is scenic, they schedule a day tour to have a quick look. And then, for many, decide to stay on for four or five days more. Some little Beach Street guest houses are cheap and charming. 'Tea and talanoa' tours give visitors a chance to sit down with a local, have a slice of banana bread, and get a first-hand account of pioneer living.

There's a museum. Shops are a delight, bras hanging in the window next to horse harnesses, shaving cream tucked in alongside a plough share, fresh fruit and ageing sundries.

At the Whale's Tale restaurant, where a large, nearly-frozen glass of fresh fruit juice made with apple, lime, mango, pineapple and pawpaw juice seems to be the choice of every table, a collection of Levuka visitors are comparing notes. It is their fourth day in town, they like it, it's very inexpensive, very *real*. Liza and Julia Ditrich, who run the main-street eatery, are partly responsible for the extended stay.

"There's lots to do now," says Liza: "you can rent mountain bikes from the YWCA, go on trekking tours into the peaks or Lovoni, take a town history tour with old Henry Sahai. There's a dive shop just down the road. People like Levuka when they finally get here."

These days, that includes passengers on the Fairstar and two Russian cruise liners. Their day in Levuka usually includes feasts, *mekes*, local entertainment. And of course once a year, there's the 'Back to Old Levuka Week' celebration, an effort not so much geared to overseas visitors, as it is to getting the rest of Fiji to remember their heritage.

Just about everybody in Fiji has got *some* link to Levuka: it seems like half the government's bigwigs went to Levuka Public School or St. John's.

Various other programmes have been tried in an effort to raise a little money. During an annual Red Cross drive, fierce looking warriors with black-painted faces throw Levuka's most prestigious people in jail ... and the community has to bail them out, the proceeds going to the charity. ("For every dollar townspeople paid to bail me out," Jennifer Brook said, "Mike paid two more dollars to keep me in.")

Another project afloat is an effort to raise money for a sea-pool. Levuka is on the water's edge, but not on a beach, and a refreshing dip in a safe pool would be nice. Safe because, with the cannery so near, the harbour waters are said to be pretty shark-intensive.

Levuka's small-town spirit is alive and well. The things that are eyesores to some are quaint to others. Some of the shops could use a coat of paint. Some have already taken advantage of special Tourism subsidies on paint if they use selected 'heritage colours'.

It doesn't really matter what paint they use: the town's local colour will always be there.

Navala, Deja Vu

The village doesn't really look any different now than it did when I first saw it 20 years ago. Which is to say that it must look about like it did, probably like *most* Fijian villages looked, one hundred years ago.

Navala Village, nearly an hour's drive into the interior from Ba, is unquestionably the most traditional, the most thatched-roofed, custom village in the entire country. And to see such stalwart preservation of tradition, such die-hard reluctance to switch to concrete and tin, is positively refreshing.

There are other villages in Fiji that have a few thatched *bures*. And there are a couple of small villages, 10 or 12 houses or so, in which most of the homes are traditionally built ... the ones that come to mind, not counting artificial cultural centres, are in the Yasawa Islands and Qamea. But nowhere in Fiji is there a village so large, so pristine, and so obviously committed to keeping the lifestyle and identity of the past.

Sitting in the darkened bure of the *turaga-ni-koro,* once again having a bowl of grog, I couldn't help feeling this was something of an anniversary. Navala revisited after 20 years. The people sitting around me couldn't help laughing when I told them about my meeting with the *turaga-ni-koro,* the village leader, back in 1975: how the old boy told me "next time you come, bring whisky".

"Oh, that was Romanu Nagata," they said. "He died."

But if Romanu asked for a non-conventional *sevusevu*, he was traditional in every other way. Navala wasn't going to bow down to modern architecture, and it certainly didn't exist for the benefit of tourists. Tourists, in his day, had to go through hell and high water to even get near the village, let alone inside the fence.

These days, the *turaga-ni-koro* has a friendlier outlook on the camera-toting visitors who are drawn to Navala's postcard-perfect setting. They can come and visit, even take some pictures, *after* they've presented their *sevusevu* and perhaps helped out a little bit with the school fund.

For the uninitiated, a *sevusevu* is the presentation of kava, *yaqona*, as the only respectful way of entering the village. The presentation is pretty much a necessity and good manners in any rural village in Fiji, but at Navala, you won't get far without it.

Twenty years ago, the road in to Navala was scenically wonderful, physically horrible. Nothing has changed. A few drastically-uphill bits have been sealed because they were so steep, cars and carriers couldn't get a grip on the dirt. But basically, the road is still steep, dusty, rough, and with a surface which sometimes looks more like a dried creek bed than anything you're used to traveling on. A four-wheel-drive vehicle with high road clearance certainly helps.

But the bumps, every spine-rattling one of them, are worth it. And they kind of creep up on you, because the road out of Ba, from Rarawai Mill into the back country, is freshly paved and smooth, the first few miles a pure delight. When it turns to dirt with single-lane bridges, some even sharing a train-track over them, you're too intent on climbing to the top of the first ridge, to that over-the-shoulder view of the sea behind, to even mind.

Black lava outcrops and cliffs line the eastern side of the road, an open expanse of non-ending hills, rocky outcrops and grasslands on the other. Sometimes there are horses on the road, sometimes cane trucks. This is a rural setting which is occasionally agricultural, more often primordial, a rough country not easily farmed or settled.

At one point, the upper end of the Ba River is visible, tucked into the dark valleys below. And suddenly, cresting a hill, Navala appears in the distance, bigger than expected, isolated by a terrain which holds no other habitation.

A river flows along one side, edging a cliff which nearly underscores the southern perimeter. There's a concrete bridge over the river, but, even here, it isn't considered good manners to stop and grab a picture. A village youth will quietly urge you to get permission first.

Navala territory extends for miles all around, so never mind a *paparazzi* technique with a telephoto lens.

I met a man named Eneriko who was just about to head off to his plantation three or four miles away. His horse was being carefully loaded with knives, axes and other tools when I pulled up alongside Navala's fence. Yes, he'd take me to the *turaga-ni-koro*, no problem, and he pulled everything down off the horse again.

How good to be back in this pandanus leaf time machine.

The only inroads to modernisation are the school and radio shed, which are, it is true, made of concrete block. They edge unobtrusively along the far side of the village, a concession to youth and education.

My brief ceremony of welcome includes the usual questions of my own vintage, number of children, wife's background, job, salary. In other parts of the world, such a CIA-style inquisition would be considered impolite, but in Fiji, it's a social palaver, no malice intended. People here just want to know everything there is to know about you.

In turn, I have been surreptitiously looking out through the open doorway, down the long green *rara* toward the river and a raised house mound which obviously, by its size and position, was a chiefly house in bygone days. Someone is leading a horse towards the river. No kids around, school's still on. There's a little layer of cloud coming up over the ridge, and if I don't get out there soon, my blue sky will be gray. I'm looking at my dusty 35 like Jesse James staring at his six-gun. Dare I pick it up and start shooting?

Eneriko, 30 or 40 minutes into his lost gardening time, is still my host, and he answers the question for me. Do I want a picture of all the people who are sharing in my *sevusevu?* Certainly. And my photo session begins.

Later, back in Suva, digging out shots of Navala taken in years past, I can see no visible difference. So little, in fact, that I can run pictures of different decades in the same article. Only the Navala people would detect the scam ... the ones who say, "*Isa*, look at little Sarafina. She's already married and has two kids ..."

Pig Hunt

Mention Robin Mercer's name anywhere in Vanua Levu and somebody will probably say something about pig hunting. It's not that the planter and developer hasn't made a mark in other endeavours. It's just that pig hunting is a more entertaining narrative.

Vanua Levu has still got a lot of thick forest. Wild country, wherein lurk wild boars.

In this enlightened day and age, folks don't look too kindly on blood sports. But, you see, Robin doesn't hunt for sport. It's a matter of request.

The boars create a lot of problems for village people. Villagers rely on subsistence farming, they grow what they need to eat, and pigs can ruin that.

"I was in one village recently, Daduilevu," Mercer said, "and the *teitei,* the garden, looked like a rugby field. The crops were flattened."

He says pig hunting was born of necessity. He moved to Vanua Levu in 1969 and built a resort. He built the house and put in the gardens, and each morning, everything he had planted the day before was gone.

No more Mr. Nice Guy.

Mercer initially tried to train Dobermans and German Shepherds to hunt pigs, but he says they were "too smart": they knew what the game was all about and stayed clear. He tried beer slops and home brew, a known planter's trick in which the pigs get *'full kasou'* , drunk as a lord, and can be easily captured. Except they weren't that easy to capture.

Next, he improvised a gun trap. And shot his own dog.

So Mercer got a bull terrier from New Zealand and crossed it with a Fiji dog. Bull terriers, he claims, keep holding on, regardless, and that's apparently important. When you have a boar backed up in the reeds and the bush is nearly impenetrable, you have to know the dog is still holding on as you cut your way into the thicket.

On this particular morning, Robin had just returned from hunting on the Yanuwai River on the north side of Natewa Bay. Four dogs in the truck, an iron spear, and "bush so thick you couldn't see a pig if it was ten feet away."

He didn't get his boar, but he did get a mind-jolting flashback. The boar crossed the road and jumped into the sea in the exact same spot where a similar pig did a similar thing years ago. That time, a bus load of villagers on the Waivunea bridge stopped, everybody screaming directions out the window, while four dogs, a boar and Mercer battled it out in the surf. He said it was "a circus".

He has other recollections. Like the time on a small island off the coast of California, on Santa Cruz, where residents were having a bad pig problem. Authorities there couldn't use dogs because the island was home to a small, endemic wild fox. So they had constructed heavy iron cages too heavy to lift, too difficult to put in place. Mercer, veteran pig hunter of the Pacific, showed them how to make simple snares using rope and a few saplings. "I made 15 snares," he said, "and after coffee, we went out and collected 9 pigs. They couldn't believe it."

And then there was the time he ended up in Savusavu hospital after he took a short cut to reach his baying hounds "up the back of Kon Tiki" and ran into a retreating boar, literally.

"It hit me and I thought, well, this is it. I remember it had bad breath, it was standing right on top of me. But one of my dogs charged in and saved me; all I got was a dislocated shoulder."

The dogs take a bit of a bashing sometimes. Mercer's favourite, a scarred old creature that couldn't be anything other than a 'pig dog', has been ripped ten or twelve times. But the old veteran is first in the truck every time they go out.

At hunt's end, a 250-pound boar on board, the meat is shared out in the village. It's great for curries, poor for lovos. Lean, almost free of fat, it is, says Mercer, a good healthy meat.

This is perhaps as good a time as any to mention that there is another side of the pig hunter. Mercer the conservationist.

A former chairman of Fiji's National Trust for a number of years, he is an authority on native birds. His own Savusavu plantation harbours 25 of Fiji's 64 species of endemic birds — and they're there because of "selective cutting and planting of native fruit trees, the feeder trees."

The time may come when he'll have to plant feeder trees for the wild pigs. And I think he'd do it, if pigs got scarce.

Floating on a Turtle's Back

I first saw 'Carapace' (it's Latin for the upper shell of a turtle) sitting high and dry on oil drums in a shipyard.

She wasn't called 'Carapace' then. I'm not even sure she had a name. But she did seem to have a lot of charm, barnacles encrusted on her bottom or not. In the short time it took to find the owner and lease the boat, I decided to give up Nasese's barking dogs, the curry-flavoured air, and the cement-block-and-vinyl-tile disaster I was renting there, forever.

I was certain I wouldn't need navigation skills. After all, the old girl's days of motoring off to Nukulau Island with a bevy of daytrippers were definitely over. No engine, for a start. But I was wrong.

True, Carapace stuck to her Bay of Islands mooring like a hermit crab to its shell. But it was the neighbours. They talked funny.

The neighbors were always talking about 'beating to windward', about gaff rigs and thingamajigs, binnacles and thingamuckles. They called a rope a sheet.

On Carapace, there are doors, windows, a kitchen, and the only sheets are on the bed. But I do not talk this way around the neighbors. They pop in at odd times, en route to shore and back in tiny dinghies, and from them, I've learned to talk nautical but nice.

And then, because we (we being my wife Sisilia, who has taken over the posts of skipper, first mate and the like) live afloat, these same neighbours expect us to do things nautical, such as tying up their dinghies when they come aboard.

"Is that *our* dinghy floating out to sea?" they ask, horrified, after handing us a 'painter' and stepping blindly inside.

So we learned to tie knots. Some of them are not in any books and they take 20 minutes to untie, but our visitors still have a dinghy when they come out.

These same neighbors automatically know not to come visiting in groups numbering more than six. This is part of living small, and the fridge can't cope with more than a dozen beers.

Actually, it would be hard to know that many neighbors, anyway. They come from Boston, Sweden, the Virgin Isles, New Zealand and all over the place. Twice a year, they move on.

Next to living small, that is the hardest part about houseboat living: everyone else can go somewhere. Carapace travels hundreds of miles each year, but it is just up and down with the tides.

The biggest thing about living small is tidiness. Buy a book - throw one out. There is absolutely no room for junk collecting. I can't even save money on Economy-Size peanut butter: the jar's too big.

But usually, whenever the urge to live in a larger house begins to surface, somebody steps aboard for the first time. Oh, what a fantastic house, they say. "Look at the view. Smell the sea air. And you really caught this fish right off the boat this morning?"

Proudly, we explain, yes, the view, the air, the fishing is good.

So what if we can't have a dog...we've got a neat aquarium right under our living room. So what if I don't have space to work? Who wants to work, anyway?

The smaller the house, the less housework. Or so it should be. Actually, boats, even floating flats, take a lot of work. Carapace is painfully in need of a little remedial cosmetics. Few ladies of her age look good without a little make-up. Perhaps next weekend. Unless it rains, because it's no good painting in the rain. And unless the sun comes out, because sunshine in Suva is so rare, it's best to take advantage of it and go out for that day.

One of the advantages of boat living, at least Carapace living, is that everything runs on gas. Lights, fridge, the works. So Suva's power cuts don't bother us: our house is lit up when all the rest of the city is dark. We don't need TV (nobody makes a gas TV) because the boat swings around on its mooring perpetually, and so the view from the living room - I mean the bridge - changes every minute or two.

Suva's Bay of Islands is so sheltered that it rarely gets much 'weather'. But when it does, Carapace, devoid of a deep hull or keel, begins to shuffle around like a tap dancer.

"What did you do in the storm?" a yachtie asked us after the last hurricane hit.. "Well," I said, trying to imitate a weathered salt, "we did the only thing possible...

"Dropped an extra fender over the side, threw out another hook, put all the breakables on the floor, took a suite in Tradewinds Hotel, ordered a dry red and rode it out.

"But it was a rough red..."

A Town Named Gizo

Hanging precariously over the bar were the skeletal remains of what once was a very large saltwater crocodile. In the height of its glory, and certainly on the day it was captured, it undoubtedly had rows of horrifying teeth, making it even more ominous than it was now.

Now, it is a conversation piece in the Gizo Hotel, a toothless relic grinning down upon my second Solbrew. It can be forgiven a sort of old croc's grin, listening to my oft-repeated vow that, of just about anywhere in the Pacific, I would be happiest living in this tiny corner of the Solomons, right here in Gizo.

Gizo people who hear this statement rarely comment on it. That means they either know that, yes, certainly nobody would want to live anywhere else, so it doesn't warrant a reply.

Or maybe they think I've had too much hot tropical sun, of which this tiny metropolis in the Western Province gets plenty. Or maybe they don't realize this is only the second Solbrew.

Anywhere else, and the comment can take some explaining. And that's the hard part: there isn't a catchy little phrase that quickly conveys the right meanings. Exactly what is it about Gizo that is so fascinating? The rusting warehouses and derelict vessels, relics of an eclipsed era? The total lack of what other centres call 'hustle and bustle'?

I like walking down the tree-shaded lanes, the seaside main drag, past the market and past rows of pleasantly inquisitive faces, knowing that I'm probably not going to get run over by one of the island's few vehicles. One of my favourite vehicles was a Landcruiser that, each year, had more wooden body parts and less metal ones, a plywood hermaphrodite and a tribute to island perseverance. It finally perished and was replaced, but the salt tang in the air will begin work on the new one.

Traffic jams in Gizo aren't on the road, they're on the beach, when a dozen or so dugout canoes line up early in the morning and fishermen begin to sell a wondrously-coloured collection of fish. Walk out to the end of any little wharf and silvery shapes, eating-size shapes, dart around in waters which are ultra-clear. Hop in a canoe and head offshore a few minutes, and there's more fish and even clearer water.

Heading offshore, incidentally, means heading in the direction of numerous other islands, all draping the horizon or spotting the middle-distance in seas which, most of the time, remain re-markably calm. Hub of government for the Western Province, canoes come in from Simbo, Ranongga and other islands with occupants intend on trading and tending to business. The market reflects the weather: good canoeing and the fruit, vegetables and fish are in generous quantity.

The market is between the shops and the government offices, next to the church, which is next to the pub. It's not a hard town to find your way around in.

I've met more interesting people in the Gizo Hotel bar than I have in any pub in the Pacific. Conversations have covered everything from the low respiration and heartbeats of a languid crocodile to the high proportion of love-related words in the Simbo dialect.

Charlie Panakera, my former drinking mate, has wandered to another part of the world, but the new proprietors are equally entertaining. They're also modernising the hotel with fancier rooms, screens instead of overhead fans and mosquito nets, but fortunately, the character, the ambience of the place remains intact.

I liked the mosquito nets: I can only hope changes are modest.

Nor should I imply that there is only one hotel. There are rest houses, some hill-top, some seaside, and a just-being-built leafhouse bar on the waterfront. Accommodation in Gizo is tropically comfortable, geckos, mosquito nets and all. You can't play at being Somerset Maugham and have an air-conditioner. Nor is it required, with Gizo's nearly constant seabreeze.

But now that Gizo is becoming the hot spot of Solomons tourism — divers and eco-tourists and folk attracted by its quaintness — the tiny berg is boasting the amenities necessary to visitor survival. There are enough shops and banking facilities to get by. There is no blue cheese, no *pouilly fuisse*. There is, instead, a sense of the planter's existence from, say, sixty years ago. You could wear a pith helmet in Gizo.

Trading boats come and go, the old style of trading boats. Wooden ships. The houses on top of the hill, some of them bastions of a colonial era, have a view of the world in all directions.

But the best view wasn't reserved for the colonialists...it was for their prisoners. Getting tossed in the clink here is to be billeted on a green and manicured hillside, catching the cooling winds off the beach.

Bakiha sites, where Gizo's earliest residents carved shell money rings from quarries of huge fossilised clam, are on the water's edge on one corner of the island.

On another corner, a line of *I Kiribati* (Gilbertese) villages provide ethnic fodder for Ron Parkinson's cultural tours, villages with an identity quite diverse from their neighbors.

There is no airstrip on Gizo. But there is an airstrip on a tiny little island about five minutes boat ride across the bay, named Nusatupe. In fact, Nusatupe isn't anything else but an airstrip, a grass runway with a boat dock. It's easy to see exactly how fighter pilots feel when they're landing on an aircraft carrier. But the Twin Otter does it with ease, landing well within the surrounding blue line. A waiting boat takes new arrivals across to the metropolis.

A self-styled Gizo exile, to be totally happy, would hinge, I suppose, on having someone who would occasionally send an interesting book. And it would depend on having a reasonable canoe with a 25 horse and a good trolling rod.

It would probably depend on having a dollar or two, not to spend foolishly on tobacco as some villagers do, but to offer to the sacrificial crocodile god over the bar.

Given these few incentives, I think I could be the Officer in Charge of Tide Measurements, Gizo Division, Western Province.

Or the official Butterfly Counter.

Waves of Malaita

Straight up, circling high on invisible thermals, twenty-five frigate birds kept tabs on the orange fibreglass canoe punching through the waves below them. Their flight was effortless and smooth. That couldn't be said of the canoe, which was smashing into the sea in a bone-jarring gallop, threatening to rip the bottom off boat and passengers alike.

The canoe ride was the tail end, pun intended, of a day-long journey from Auki to Wairokai and back, which before it was over, would include four hours of bumping along in the back of a truck and three more as a spray-covered, shaken and well-mixed mariner.

But then, this was Malaita, and a spirit of adventure was not only a good idea, it was a total necessity. No Sheratons, tour buses and club cars in this neck of the woods, and a refrigerated drink is rarer than porpoise teeth.

The truck was arranged by the Malaita Provincial Council and the bumpy travel was self-inflicted: I chose to ride in the open for a better view of the surroundings, a faster draw with my loaded Nikon. The air was early-morning fresh, the road so devoid of traffic that dust wasn't a problem. I kept noting the rich and thick smell of vegetation which in turn aroused memories of other dense jungles, of Bougainville particularly. At that hour of the morning, school kids were just beginning to pour out onto the road, some to walk for five minutes, some for five miles.

And that was when I discovered a truly interesting thing. Wave at these children with a big, arms-out wave and you got a big, arms-out wave back. A flick of the wrist with a thumbs up sign and, presto, a dozen beaming schoolchildren flicked their wrists and stuck their thumbs up.

This duplicating symbol of gladness worked through an hour's worth of variations, some of them giddishly comical. By 8 am, the kids were all in school and I had to look for other attractions.

Malaita is nearly 200 km long, and I was in the process of traveling half that, intent on mentally noting (on these roads, you sure as heck can't *write* anything) all the things that make this part of the Pacific so jungle-like and unspoiled. Like pictures in a 1950 National Geographic, a time warp of unchanged lifestyles, except the current pictures were brighter.

The Malaita experience had begun right at the airport, at Gwaunaruu, where a sizable and very traditional village butts right up against the landing strip.

Now I was barreling down a road which was crushed white coral. With a little moon, it would be a wonderful road to travel at night, almost self-lighting. The sides were lined with kapok trees, sago palms and huge hardwoods which must have begun their reach for the sky eons ago. They had bright red lichen-covered trunks and an aerial assault of vines and creepers. Some of those trees had such splendidly vaned supports with such precise symmetry that they looked like rockets on a launching pad. Bird sounds filtered through the green mesh.

At Kwainaketo Village just outside Auki, I pounded on the truck's roof to arrange a stop. A tree house there looked like something out of the past, a left-over from an era when tree shelters housed guards and lookouts and offered a defensive vantage point over attackers. This one had been created by village youth for fun.

But every village from Kwainaketo onwards was a thatched one, an un-changing Pacific landscape here, but a difficult one to find these days in many other island countries. Malaita is rugged and intensely forested, with mountain streams crossing the road at regular intervals, water hazards the Council's Hilux took without a pause. The crossings invariably seemed to be filled with small children swimming or playing in canoes and women washing clothes.

Malaita has the largest population of any island in the Solomons and for the person who has time to get way out in the bush, the rewards would be rich, indeed. Culturally, the island has a lot to offer: man-made islands in the lagoons; a people with traditions of shark calling, kite fishing and ancestor worship; and a still very-much-alive commerce in manufacturing shell money. I wasn't going to have the time to get really lost. In fact, at the speed this truck was moving, I might not have time for anything.

My vantage point in the back of the Hilux was less productive than expected. Scenes were changing so quickly that glimpses of things photographic - and there were many of them - were gone again before I could bang on the truck top. Clean and well-managed gardens; women on the road with mighty burdens of firewood cradled on their heads; and Malaita's trade-mark, children with golden hair and back-lit halos almost everywhere I looked.

At road's end, a canoe was supposed to be waiting. We were carrying the fuel for it in the back of the truck. But the canoe had gone somewhere else. A setback? Not really. Another was organised, a price agreed on, and before I was even ready, I was beginning the trip to Wairokai.

There was barely time to pictorially capture a very shy girl on a very long stony beach, who coyly twisted in opposite directions trying to elude the lens. The villagers, just about all of them, hooted and rolled on the ground and they were still laughing when I was well offshore.

Just offshore, the sea was pounding hard. Two hours later, a sheltered opening seemed pure heaven; Wairokai was just behind the mangroves. The journey was a long one and I'd already adjusted to the idea it might not be possible to return to Auki the same day. My host, Luke Susuta, gave me a guided inspection of the village, pointing out the long house 'dorm' where I would be staying, and the beds made up of five or six slender poles, four inch gaps between the sticks, and the upraised end that slants the whole arrangement at a 20-degree angle off the hard floor. It was difficult to imagine that anyone could sleep on one.

"Well, Luke," I said, "I've gotta be heading back to the boat."

I'd actually come this far to interview Luke Susuta — 'Uncle Luke' as he's called on radio, the pidgin story-teller who, weekly, has enthralled Solomon Islands Broadcasting Commission's audiences for about 35 years.

Retirement and village-life didn't put an end to his weekly yarns: it just meant Luke had to record a dozen at a time and ship them back to Honiara.

Without planning it, I'd timed my village entrance to coincide with one of Luke's radio broadcasts. Everyone at Wairokai, and apparently just about everywhere else the SIBC reaches, was listening in. Hopefully, some of them had radios with fresher batteries.

Luke gets his stories from the mail, parcels of them from people everywhere in the Solomons. Luke reads them, puts them aside, then retells them. True stories aren't very interesting and are rarely funny, he says. He likes funny stories. "A man goes fishing and pulls up a crocodile. That is funny. Or he goes fishing and spends all day pulling and pulling, but at the end of the day, he finally pulls in a big black stone. You see? Funny stories..."

The trip back was faster, the canoe surfing with a following sea. Birds were everywhere, charting the course of tuna beneath them. My lethargy was shaken by a manta ray which twice leapt out of the water, somersaulted, and smacked down hard on the surface, close enough to photograph if I'd been able to get the cameras out of the plastic bread bags fast enough. Which I wasn't.

I was back in Auki at dusk, just in time to nip down to a Chinese store and pick up a cold beer, and in time to sit on the verandah of the Auki Lodge and drink it. The Auki Lodge is the only visitor facility on Malaita, and I'd remembered a time several years back when the Lodge had run out of water, didn't have any food, and had very little else to recommend it. It's changed. A cook is in place, there's a chicken on the grill, a leaf-house dining room has been constructed and a white picket fence surrounds its domain. In the gardens, a flowering tree dropped petals which formed brilliant red pools along the path.

Auki is Malaita's big smoke, the provincial capital. During the day, the smoke is, well, fairly hard to see. But in the cool evening air, Auki was coming alive. People were strolling down to the wharf, playing soccer, and making last sales before the market fence was locked. It was blissfully unbusy.

I had arranged transport to pick me up an some ungodly hour so that I could head down the coast in the morning. I wanted to see Langa Langa Lagoon and the man-made islands in the lagoon's centre. The islands were erected generations ago by piling reef stones on the shallow mud flats. Supposedly, they offered some protection against headhunters. It was difficult to see exactly how...time to see them coming and kiss your head goodbye? But more importantly, the islands are out of range of most of the malaria-breeding mosquitoes.

Langa Langa Lagoon is a major centre for boatbuilding and I could count at least five vessels up on the slips, some mere ribs awaiting planking, some almost seaworthy. But traditionally, the fame of the area lies in its shell-money production, with the red and white bivalve *Spondylus* painstakingly rounded, shaped, drilled and tied into multi-strand lengths called *tafuliae*, used for chiefly gifts and bride payments.

Laulasi Village, at the centre of the lagoon, makes a business of being nice to visitors. A real business, because it charges more than a Disneyland ticket to tread its man-made shores. If it hadn't been for the girl with the tri-line tattoo, an elaborate marking which looked almost like Air New Zealand's Maori motif, elegantly enhanced by her Malaitan smile, it wouldn't have been worth it.

Savo Sorcery

Thick vines, snake-like green creepers, massive tree trunks and dense bush surround the tiny village of Legalau, but it's the sounds as much as the forest wall that makes this place so unique.

It's like the audio-track of a Tarzan movie, a collection of squawks, warbles, screeches and other bird noises emanating from the greenery in such rich profusion that it would be an ornithologist's Mecca.

Legalau is one of the fifteen villages on the volcanic island of Savo, across Iron Bottom Sound from Honiara.

On this particular morning, the seas were so glassy that sky and ocean edge merged, the horizon disappeared, and a distant ship coming into port was suspended in a gray featureless void. Floating in space. The plop of flying fish re-entering the water was audible even above the drone of the outboard. In just over an hour, Juvence Selevale's canoe was hitting Legalalau's beach.

The Tourism Council of the South Pacific helped set the village up as a 'nature site village', a low-key self-help project. As visitor destinations go, there are some bigger. Legalau has two guest cottages and can take up to six people at one time. It was fully booked when I got there: five people who had come to try it out for a day or two and were staying for ten. It is a clean and landscaped retreat cut out from the bush on a low plateau above the sea.

Food is totally island style - fish, cassava, cabbage and fruit - but TCSP funding assisted with some refinements such as a fridge and real toilets.

The surprise was in finding Savo, so close to Honiara, such a natural and unspoiled showcase of custom and tradition. If I had any doubts on that aspect, they were quickly dismissed when Ben Duva, Legalau's host, informed me the village girls were 'painting up' for a custom dance. 'Village girls' doesn't necessarily mean girls: it can include a lot of old hens as well, but the dance group assembling was a pretty fine team. I was beginning to feel sorry, already, that the two leaf-huts were booked out.

Shell-money strings and porpoise-teeth headbands gyrating nicely over their oiled bodies, the dancers performed with style and fervor.

Voices of the dancers are relatively shrill — it's a harmony that would take some getting used to. On the other hand, people here might find Jessye Norman or soprano Sarah Brightman's voices an acquired taste.

The birds in the forest were still competing with the chants from the ladies; I could smell roasting cassava coming from the leaf houses. This was a good setting for a visiting naturalist, and the real drawing card would be a trek to the megapod nesting beach, or a junket to either of Savo's two active volcanoes. The megapods are a short distance away and best observed in the cool hours, early in the morning or just before dusk. Megapods lay their eggs in thermal vents and let the naturally-heated terrain do the work of incubation. They pick spots which are not too hot, not too cold.

Smart birds.

Savo's thermal vents include a steaming hot-spring easily accessible by canoe along the northern coast, and a bigger cauldron inland that is more of a hike.

Ben Duva and a 12-year-old boy named Mak had come across from Savo early in the morning, picking me up alongside the Navy Yard in Honiara. The TCSP venture was on Ben's land, and he had applied for the concession after six other Savo applications were rejected. Some had apparently been too close to schools or too near villages and so Ben had said, well, maybe you should come and look at my place.

Mak, unofficial guide and camera-carrier, was keeping a low-profile during the dances (all those yucky girls) but was on his feet instantly when we started off in search of megapods. It was already too late in the day, the sun too warm and we were unsuccessful. (Mad dogs and Englishmen, maybe, but not the level-headed and big footed megapod).

The sun *was* hot. But I didn't have much choice: Legalau's visitor facilities were full and I had to return to Honiara. Mak, sun reflecting off his golden hair, wanted to make his second trip of the day.

I was curious what happens when the seas get too rough for comfort, but Ben said, in those conditions, the boat went straight across to the northern tip of the Guadalcanal coast, a journey of only seven miles compared to the thirty miles to Honiara. A truck or bus would then take people into town.

The horizon had returned, a distinct line where the ocean ended.

I was still looking back at Savo, raving in fact to Ben and Mak about what a good place it was. "You just liked the bare-breasted girls," Ben chided. "I didn't notice," I said.

"Many years ago, most people in the Solomons were very frightened of the Savo people. We were known as poison-men and sorcerers, sun-worshippers who were so fearful that mothers used to walk on their children's tracks to cover them from the sorcerer's eyes."

"You probably wouldn't have come, then," said Ben, "or left your footprints in Savo sand."

The Ghostly Guest House

One thing about flying to Kirakira is that you sure see a lot of Guadalcanal. The flight path runs from Henderson Field all the way down the length of the island, an aerial view of what is obviously unspoiled wilderness. Unspoiled because it's so incredibly mountainous and rugged.

Kirakira itself is, well, just one of those stations. The usual health centre and Telekom dish, the post office and police post, a few canoes pulled up on the beach by the market. Gigantic rain trees cover the roads with a green canopy. Children were singing in loud and clear voices from one of the schools, and the tractor driver was saying that if I managed to get out to the Three Sisters islands, the reef fishing there was really pretty good.

The tractor driver takes the place of what, in Hawaii, might be the airport limo. Sitting on the trailer just behind the tractor, though, provides a far more comprehensive view of the banyan trees and harbour than you could ever get in a limousine, and the ride to town is pretty short, anyway. Just long enough to hear that the Three Sisters also have a lot of saltwater crocs living in the lagoons. So thick with them that a Japanese film crew came all the way to Kirakira just to film them.

Which is all fine and dandy, except my style of fishing is to find a quiet little spot ankle deep at the reef's edge and toss a line into the deep water with a spinning rod and a small octopus lure.

Saltwater crocodiles could spoil my cast.

Kirakira was approaching. I could tell, because the tractor was coming to a stop. At the entrance to town, just across the one-lane bridge which the tractor tyres cleared by a good two inches, was a Friary. As in Friar Tuck, not as in Colonel Sanders. And beyond that was the village green with a custom house in its centre, complete with carved totems. There used to be a Kirakira Club alongside the custom house, where, I suppose, the area's planters quaffed their gin and tonics, but it no longer exists. Good thing, too ... we wouldn't want the town to become known as a bawdy, rowdy den of revelry and insalubrity.

I was just a little worried about finding some story material. Short of saltwater crocodiles, which were a bit too far away to reach before the aircraft returned from Santa Cruz to collect me, I was looking at a very green and clean station, but one which was about as quiet as a butterfly carnival. What's that old Zen thing, about the sound of one hand clapping?

"Where do people stay," I asked, "if they do come here?"

"Well," said my host, "the government has a rest house, but it's pretty much for people on official government business. The old one, the ghost house, is empty."

It was probably my hearing. He probably said guest house.

"Yes," said Jack. "Nobody stays in the guest house any more..."

"...the ghost ran them all out."

Things were looking up. Was this ghostly guest house far away? Not at all, said Jack. "It's right there."

These days, the guest house serves as an art gallery for village youth. The steps have nearly fallen away and the entrance is boarded over, but a peep inside is entertaining. Kids here take anatomy seriously. Rate the gallery 'Adults Only'. Whatever happened to hearts and arrows with 'Tom loves Becky' and that sort of thing?

But what happened here after 1927, the year the big old colonial house was built, might have had some hearts and arrows after all. Jack Campbell told me all about the house, and it could involve a love story of sorts.

The government station was to have a house for the resident District Officer. A site was chosen, and a big banyan tree in the middle of it had to be cut down. The ghost lived in that banyan tree. She even had a name, and her name was Kapino. There are several versions of just why Kapino lived in the banyan tree. One was that she was a jilted lover, and she took her life in the tree, hanging herself after an argument with her true love. Another version is that she was incurably ill, and that she was left in the tree to die. Village elders seem to think the latter version is the correct one.

So the tree was cut, the house was built, and the first District Officer, a chap named Parker, took up residence. The ghost ran him out of the house, although he stayed quite a bit longer than others.

The ghost, say those in the know, felt that, OK, you cut down my house so I'll live in yours.

Kapino, it seems, only bothered Europeans, and only men. If a woman was around the house, everything was hunky-dory. But a man on his own, and things started getting funny as fast as the sun would set. Boots would unlace themselves, ping-pong balls would fly around the room, water taps would come on, and books and belongings started to be ambulatory when there wasn't any logical explanation why they should be moving.

"How many people saw this ghost?" I asked Jack. "Three, four...?"

"Oh, nobody has ever seen her," he said. "But she's pestered over a dozen men. They weren't actually chased out of the house, they were pestered out. There was a District Officer who spent his entire contract at my father's house...wouldn't come near this place. When my father would go to investigate, there wasn't a sound or a murmur."

The ghost, now, is quiet. Probably because there isn't anybody in the house to bother. Jack says it's her house, now, and it's probably more comfortable than the tree.

I had another look through the door. Kind of spooky, all right. The drawings on the walls looked a bit rough, but I guess Kapino is a fairly liberated lady.

But I bet Kirakira's kids don't do much drawing in there at night.

The Second Invasion of Guadalcanal

Marines in full battle dress stood by the roadside, heads bowed in prayer. Lines of military trucks, some of them ex-Operation Desert Storm, pushed their way through the tall kunai grass near the Bloody Ridge marker. Landing craft launched from naval ships in the bay plowed through the waves to shore, landing not at Red Beach but at the Point Cruz Yacht Club.

Honiara was a city besieged, and this second invasion of Guadalcanal took the Solomons by storm.

One thousand Allied war veterans, some of them still wearing dog-tags around their necks, gathered on August 7, 1992, to remember the Guadalcanal Campaign, launched fifty years earlier when the US 1st Marine Division landed on Red Beach.

The 50th Anniversary of the Battle of Guadalcanal should rightly have been called the 50th Remembrance. Anniversary seems an inappropriate word for what is described as World War II's bloodiest and longest campaign, six months of action in which 16 Allied ships were sunk, 1023 American and Australian sailors lost, and 1600 United States Marines killed. Japanese losses were more severe: 23,000 men killed, 25 ships sunk.

The military presence for this remembrance was not all geriatric. Three naval ships in port off-loaded scores of uniformed and gung-ho young men; truck convoys of Marines in battle dress readied ceremonial cites; a tent camp sprung up next to the police barracks.

The influx left Honiara's residents in awe. They stood roadside all the way to Henderson field, waving at passing motorcades. Old scouts and island veterans, medals proudly flashing in the sun, made their way into town. The entire populace ducked as a ground-hugging fighter jet, an F-111, screamed over the capital, scaring the pants off half the kids in town.

If the delta-wing made the local children cry, their ex-Scout grandfathers were wiping tears from their own eyes at first one flag ceremony and then another.

World War II was being re-lived in detail, with marathon speeches delivered in a merciless sun at three different memorial sites.

Flags were raised, wreaths laid. Honour guards swayed in the heat and were handed discreet cups of water. Stories unfurled around every gathering: "Hell, there sure wasn't a bridge at Lungga in those days...of the nine men in my mortar squad, only two survived...the artillery cover saved our necks. They laid rounds twenty-five feet ahead of us, so accurate you could light a cigarette by holding it over your head..."

Everyone had a story, and some names were a focal point of all of them: Galloping Horse Ridge, the Gifu, Bloody Ridge, Alligator Creek, Kakambona, Tenaru and Matanikau.

In 1942, the number of soldiers entrenched in Guadalcanal was higher than the number of people living in the islands. And the Solomon Islanders were caught in the middle. Had they divided their support for both sides, the outcome could very possibly have been different.

"Guadalcanal," said General J.R. Dailey, Assistant Commandant of the Marine Corps in Honiara for the event, "was the turning point of the war in the Pacific."

It was also the Marine Corps' longest engagement in World War II, and the Corps' first large-scale amphibious landing.

By mid-February, 1942, the Japanese evacuated 13,000 men, the only survivors of 36,000 that landed on Guadalcanal, and the Battle for Guadalcanal was over.

Over, that is, except in the minds of the veterans who were reliving it in painstaking detail.

James Smith, Dick MacNeilly and Harman Hunt, members of the volunteer 1st Marine Raiders Battalion, wore their skull insignia as a mark of extreme pride, the dare-devil elite within the elite.

"We were a good bunch," noted Smith. "Our battalion produced seven generals and the US Navy named 24 ships after our men."

Bill McCormack, 182nd Infantry, was celebrating his 21st birthday on December 26, 1942. He remembers thinking that, as birthdays go, it was a heck of a mess. And then a mortar shell hit the beach a few feet away from him and he "lost 17 fillings in my teeth from the concussion."

Colonel George Cole, at 91 the oldest vet at the anniversary, was a life-long trooper who remembers not only the Japanese in the Solomons, but fighting Sandinos in Nicaragua. He first got his taste for adventure as a 19-year-old wing-walker on stunt biplanes barn-storming the United States.

The ceremonies at Skyline Ridge, Rove and the Henderson Field/Edson's Ridge marker resulted in cracked voices and tears in some, solemn salutes from others. But few were left unmoved.

In town, lines of bright-eyed children stretched across the wharf for a chance to go aboard the USS Racine or HMAS Tobruk, or to be hoisted atop tanks and landing craft displayed on the wharf alongside.

Veterans walking through the jam-packed hotels studied insignias, name tags and faces, looking for any indication that this might have been the fellow in the next foxhole.

There were about 20 Fiji veterans standing in parade rank as well. At the end of a five-hour memorial service, a van load of sulu-clad Fijians headed for China Town to scout out some lunch. Poking his nose into a likely-looking establishment, one of them shouted back "Time spent on reconnaissance is seldom wasted."

A thousand Allied veterans, some bedecked with medals, some undecorated, humble fighting men. But almost all had one decoration in common: white hair. For these beer-bellied, baseball-capped warriors, there won't be time for another anniversary like this one.

Bloody Ridge and Plum Pudding

Children were fishing off the bridge at Alligator Creek, a bevy of beaming faces eager to display their wriggling, silver catch. At the mouth of the creek, where it joins Iron Bottom Sound, about 20 fishing canoes raced the morning sun, a wooden armada gathered broadside in a miniature replay of another flotilla 50 years earlier. And by late afternoon, a hay-stack topped girl, wild yellow hair in stark contrast to her darker skin, was standing in the red glow of sunset on Bloody Ridge, fingers tracing a bronze plaque in case I hadn't noticed.

Everywhere I went, I was walking on hallowed ground, and the signs of the war were everywhere — barges on the beaches, Bailey-bridge steel around the gardens; helmets, rifle barrels and other rusting mementos on shelves and walls of restaurants and other incongruous places.

Signs of the war are also nowhere. A new arrival to Guadalcanal would find it difficult to locate some of the names from history. Trying to find the Gifu, Galloping Horse Ridge, Red Beach and Bloody Ridge, the Sherman tank in the coconut plantation or the amphibious tractors off Tetere Bay isn't easy.

I was on an eight-day assignment to scout around for people still alive who'd played a part in the war, the 'Big Death' as the Solomon Islanders call it, and to photograph the war relics and visual artifacts that had survived 50 years of tropical humidity.

But it wasn't really the humidity that got to me.

It was the humility: the 'banzai' jokes in the rented jeep, the comfortable ease with which two of us began our patrol of the ridge. And then, actually being on top of this low, feature-less spine where so many fighting men died, the overpowering force of a thousand ghosts. Tread lightly.

Humbled, the drive back to the main road was completed without a word being spoken.

The map I got from the Lands Department was last corrected in 1988 and still bore the stamp of the British Solomon Islands Protectorate. But it had battle grounds marked with a logo of a bayonet-thrusting soldier, and a collection of pencilled circles where various people suggested I might find things of interest — the cave-like entrance to the underground hospital next to the new Lungga bridge; the memorials to Marines and Japanese, side-by-side, atop Mount Austen. Certainly I should view the relics at Vilu War Museum and visit Betikama Mission.

The map eased the frustration I'd had spending two fruitless days searching the bush where I *thought* things should have happened, so easily pinpointed now that I had a map in hand. Thick grass and shading trees hide the 30 or so amphibious tractors on Tetere Bay, American landing craft whose usefulness ended when the shore was gained. A Sherman tank guards a coconut plantation within shell-range of the partially-exposed *Kinugawa Maru* and *Hirokawa Maru,* 15 minutes drive west of Honiara. The airfield lookout tower on Henderson Field is a daring playground for village kids who scale the steel girders with the agility of a Spitfire scaling the clouds.

Guadalcanal's irrefutable memorials are mostly underwater. Iron Bottom Sound is named for the scores of American and Japanese ships sunk in the horrendous sea battle between Savo Island and the mainland, but the seas here are deep. So deep that very sophisticated equipment is required to breach this museum.

A National Geographic-endorsed team headed by Bob Ballard, the leader of both the *Titanic* and *Bismarck* discovery operations, located and identified 10 ships in Iron Bottom Sound before mechanical problems on the search vessel temporarily ended the quest. He would return in June to continue the search, this time hoping to add J.F. Kennedy's torpedo boat, PT 109, to his list. The PT boat is resting somewhere between Gizo and Kolombangara in the Western Province.

I went West, too, scanning not only New Georgia's war-time airfields at Seghe and Munda, but searching for more elusive quarry, the scouts. Local villagers were recruited by the Americans to serve as guides, coastwatchers, intelligence personnel and, occasionally, as part of the fighting force.

Within minutes of checking into the Gizo Hotel, the hotelier, Charlie Panakera, was telling me about one of Kennedy's principal rescuers, Aaron Kumana. The scout was at Koqu Village on Ranongga Island.

And before the evening was out, I'd met Gizo dive operator Danny Kennedy, whose fascination with 50-year-old war memorabilia is enhanced by the fact that most divers coming to the

Western Province want to explore war wreckage, of which there's plenty. Danny regularly takes his clientele to drop in on a Japanese transport ship, the *Toa Maru;* to American Hellcats and a Corsair, all at depths of fewer than 30 metres. He has become enough of an authority to become the liaison with the National Geographic team, particularly in regard to the PT 109 episode.

Danny had been told Aaron was dead. Charlie Panakera said he saw him in town two days ago, selling betel nut in the market. We set off in a fibreglass canoe to find out.

Two hours later, we were sitting in Koqu Village and Aaron was sitting in front of us. But he said he wasn't going to have any pictures taken and he wasn't going to tell a story. John Kennedy, he said, was dead and so there was no *reason* to tell the story. Period. It took two hours of delicate negotiations before this wizened veteran in a purple laplap, his dog-tag proudly hanging from his neck, would consent to the camera's intrusion.

Back in Gizo, other stories began to emerge. Charlie said that, each year from 1986 to 1992, a group of Japanese businessmen came to his hotel, chartered a small aircraft, and flew over neighboring Vella Lavella. With a loudspeaker blaring the Imperial anthem, they dropped thousands of plastic cards over the island, saying, 'Come out, you are national heroes.' A rumour kept circulating that the Vella Levalla people had seen 'Chinamen' (Japanese) in ragged clothes hiding in the hills. The seven year campaign was unfruitful: the last soldiers of the Empire never emerged and sceptics said they were never there.

Charlie introduced his dad, Simon Panakera, supposedly already 42 years old when the war reached Gizo. As a scout in the Seghe area of New Georgia, he "saw plenty of Japanese." Then quietly added "Mi siutim plenti."

Danny Kennedy started talking about a top-secret American plane, a remote-controlled dive bomber, sitting perfectly intact in the Shortlands, between Bougainville and Papua New Guinea. But there was lots of other interesting things around. In fact, if I wanted to forego my plane ticket to Munda, he'd take me there by canoe. Which would result in photographs, he said, of some never-before-photographed weaponry in the bush.

Nine hours of intense Solomon sunshine later, I was cursing the canoe's hard seat and at the same time rejoicing that I had super photographs of an American 13-ton tank at Tahitu in such perfect shape that, except for the hole from a 37 mm anti-tank shell which went right through the driver's seat, looked like you could charge the battery and crank her over. Machine guns which still swiveled. Hard black rubber still in place on her treads.

At Enoghae, he showed me four 140 mm coastal guns, their range spanning the gulf between New Georgia and Kolombangara. And at Boeboe Village in Vona Vona Lagoon, another Kennedy-era scout, Moses Sesa, held a signed picture of JFK himself, a 'thank-you' from the President-to-be.

I would have about five hours in Munda at daybreak to track down four names: Biuku Gasa, Jimmy Bennett, Eddie Wickham and Alfred Basili. But Alfred was already waiting for me as I got out of the canoe. Word seems to travel fast in this chain of islands.

Biuku, the man most frequently mentioned in relation to PT

109, wasn't likely to talk to me, Alfred explained. He was tired of talking to people who made him promises and then gave him nothing. And besides, he lived two hours away by boat and I wouldn't have time to see him. Jim Bennett had a shop at the airstrip — but hadn't come in for the last few days.

So I listened to Alfred Basili's tale of being caught by the Japanese and being released on the proviso he told all the other villagers to leave the area; of scouting with Jim Bennett and being provided with firearms and grenades by the 43rd Infantry.

These days, he is the area tour guide for war veterans of both sides, something he's been doing for twenty years. "Once a Japanese man was on my tour, and I showed him a Japanese pillbox at the end of Munda airstrip. I told him that, in the days when I was armed and with Bennett, I told the Japanese to come out and surrender. They were very brave. They would not come out. So I put a mortar shell into that pillbox. Every man but one was killed. The man I was showing it to said, "Yes, I know. I was in that bunker.' But today we are friends."

Before Danny headed back to Gizo, he introduced me to another dive operator, Dave Cooke, a blond-haired Brit who agreed to continue where Danny left off. We'd just have time, he figured, to get to Kennedy's PT base at Lubaria Island before my scheduled departure.

The sea between Munda and Rendova is so clear and so teeming with fish, that a dive operation here seems like a very sensible way to make a living. Cooke takes people to the dump. Dropping in on the dump means the American dump at the end of the airstrip, an underwater showcase where Jeeps, motorcycles, guns, ammo and Coke bottles lie in abundance.

"You Yanks didn't go to war without Coca-Cola did you," chides Dave. The Coke legacy is further enhanced at Lubaria, where a village community project has erected a PT Base museum. The ocean floor around the island is apparently littered with the multi-faced green bottles, all marked 1942. I am now the proud owner of one. Maybe JFK himself tossed it in the drink before setting out on that fateful encounter off Plum Pudding Island.

Kennedy was, though, but one man. Sometimes it's worthwhile to remember that the names and deeds of countless scouts and fighting men were largely unrecorded. They did what they were supposed to do, including dying, without so much as a mention.

The 50th Anniversary of the Battle of Guadalcanal was approaching. By the time the next great anniversary comes around, there'll be very few participants alive to tell the tale. And yet, the legacy of war won't end that fast.

An Australian ordnance demolition squad claims to have 30 years of work ahead of it. Bar conversations, too, will continue as they always do.

"...did you know, they've just found a Zero wrapped in canvas and clean as a whistle at Santa Isabel..."

"...we'd been going up and down that track for years on the way to the beach. The dog took five steps off the track and, WHOOM."

For years to come, men will be paying homage to the spirits on the Ridge. For both sides.

Cloud Sailing on a 1941 Flying Boat

I couldn't help being intrigued. For one thing, we're both just about exactly the same vintage. We've both got 1941 engines.

She's a three-passenger Republic SeaBee, probably the only flying boat still commercially operating in the entire Pacific, a working relic.

I was gazing at her bulbous hull and freshly-painted 1947 airframe, and the fascination must have been obvious because her owner came over, justifiably proud of this veteran craft, and offered me a ride from Henderson Field to Tulagi and back.

Sure thing, I said, and secretly nurtured a hope that the SeaBee ran better than I did.

And it did.

Single engine pushing instead of pulling, the SeaBee lumbered down Henderson Field and turned due north toward the Solomon's first capital. A small toggle switch in the instrument panel read 'Bilge Pump'. Hmmm. Can't be too many aircraft flying around these days with a bilge pump in them.

Then, owner and pilot, pleased as punch at showing off what I reckoned was a new toy, levered the wheels up. This particular process kept his right arm busy most of the way, pumping a hydraulic lever which locked the wheels below us into storage. We were now ready for a proper sea landing, with a hull instead of wing floats.

That landing was as smooth as a spoon scraping pudding. Tulagi's harbour was like glass, and the v-shaped hull cut through with a gentle whoosh. A small wharf by a large container ship seemed the only refuge, and as we neared, a crowd of Tulagi villagers stood in unabashed mirth.

The SeaBee *is* a little funny looking.

One of the people on the wharf, still staring at the boat after I'd opened the front hatch and climbed out, said 'plen blong bifo, tru' — a plane from earlier times, all right.

Dick Grouse, Heli Solomon's managing director, bought the SeaBee from a Queensland doctor and flew it from Australia, leapfrogging from Brisbane to Horn Island, Port Moresby to Milne Bay, Misima to Munda, and then on to Honiara.

It was built by the Republic Aircraft Corporation, the same company that made the World War II vintage P-47 Thunderbolt.

Did he buy it for a toy, a collector's keepsake? I asked. No way, Grouse said. The SeaBee is a working plane, an answer to a country with relatively few airstrips and infrequent shipping, but with quite a few calm harbours, lagoons and land-locked lakes.

He also hinted that, while technically the engine housing says 1941, the work horse (sea horse?) in this craft was re-worked and re-engineered until it was almost new.

So I began to feel better. If it seemed to purr a little smoother than I do in my usual uphill race, I shouldn't feel ashamed at losing the race. It's been rebuilt; I haven't.

SOLOMON ISLANDS: Malaita's (179) blond-haired children, tidy villages and 'shell-money' culture vie with Western Province diving as the strongest island attractions.

SOLOMON ISLANDS -
The town of Gizo (175) in
the Western Province still
seems to warrant a pith
helmet. Gizo children
check out diver Danny
Kennedy's reflexes (198).

SOLOMON ISLANDS - Shy, oh so shy (179); Greg Blanchette and 'Triangle Island' (227); pre-dance cosmetics on Savo Island (186); I'Kiribati (219) in Titiana Village; Story-teller Luke Susuta, Wairakai, (179).

SOLOMON ISLANDS - Signs of war (198) are everywhere; ageing scouts Aaron Kumana and Moses Sese (198); Modern-day Marines (194) pay tribute to comrades who fell 50 years earlier.

SOLOMON ISLANDS - A "haystack-topped girl" (198) on the crest of Bloody Ridge; a survey ship continues to probe the depths of Iron Bottom Sound, searching for a sunken fleet (198); Vilu War Museum (198) and the relics of 'Skull Island' during its cannibal era (223).

PAPUA NEW GUINEA - Most colourful
of island nations when it comes to
custom dance, 'PNG' has 700 language
groups and a huge ethnic diversity.

SOLOMON ISLANDS - The author on
Savo Island (186): just another hard
day in the office.

Munda Magic

It must be one of the few places in the world where the plane taxis into the very centre of town. At the end of the runway, the Twin Otter turns right and motors down a paved lane into Munda, the heart of New Georgia, the sixth biggest island in the Solomons.

The police station, 'Ag' offices and other government buildings are all around. One and a half minutes walk away is the hotel, the dive centre and the sea.

Munda conveys an almost instant feeling of peace and well-being. The air smelled fresh and clean and cicadas were running through their morning drill.

I dropped a light travel bag in the sand alongside the road (not too many places you could do *that*, either) and strolled down the seaside lane. Each house had two or three canoes, not all of them usable. As I walked, I could hear Tina Turner coming from a radio in one of the leaf houses. Everybody that passed me on the road smiled and said 'good morning' When I turned to go back, heading toward Agnes Lodge, I ran into an old friend, George Cook, who was patching a hole in a fibreglass boat.

George hardly said hullo before he swung into his favourite topic: how good this part of the world was. "You know," he said, "I've probably made the crossing between Gizo and Munda a hundred times in a canoe and I've never yet gotten tired of it.

How could you take this for granted...where else have you got fish jumping out of the sea into your boat?"

He pointed his paint-splattered fingers at a fellow who was just hauling a catch of bright red fish out of a canoe and on to the dock, and just as quickly, somebody from the Lodge was shouting to kitchen staff to pick out three or four for dinner.

Agnes Lodge has twenty-five beds, some of them in an air-conditioned new wing, but somehow, being in 'fancy' accommodation just wouldn't seem right. This little pub has lots of character about it, and the waters of Roviana Lagoon lapping alongside. It was once a 3-bedroom rest house for government employees, but when government got tired of running it, the cook bought it.

That was in 1975 and the cook was Agnes Kera. Two sons and a son-in-law have helped her with the effort, but it's sprightly, bubbly, 75-year-old Agnes that provides the glow in the garden. I tried to get her to confess she must be a Solomons version of Michener's Bloody Mary, but she denied it: the rest house was always quiet, no drinks in those days, the officers who came through were always well-behaved.

A veteran at the Lodge explained that Agnes "was always popular with the officers, because right after the war, she could get eggs and bacon when nobody else could."

Agnes has ten children, 70 grandchildren. "All those kids running around here are related to me," she said, with a wave of her hand. "German, English, Gilbertese, Malaita, all of them." And then she got up and went back into the laundry, where she'd been since 6:30 in the morning.

The first plane each morning brings with it the newspaper, and within minutes of the aircraft's arrival, knots and clusters of people are congregating on the main street to share the news. Munda isn't a big circulation area for the Solomons Star or the Voice: it looks like ten people take turns reading each paper. At the same time, children are coming back from the bakery with a hot loaf under their arm. An old scout in a well-worn army jacket invites me to sit with him by the road for a while and offers a fresh betel nut from his collection.

It's a Munda sort of day.

Splat! - The Ubiquitous Betel Nut

Legends speak of streets paved with gold. The Beatles sang of a Yellowbrick Road. But Honiara's streets are neither yellow nor gold. They're paved with red, and for that we have to thank not the Beatles but betel nut.

Visitors arriving from parts of the world where a certain tall palm does not grow, could be mistaken for thinking those fearful red splotches are bloodstains.

But their concern is erased when, five feet away from them, another red stain adds its colour to the dusty soil between road and sidewalk. Its creator is a grinning old veteran who was probably chewing betel nut when the Japanese came. His teeth are jet black, the inside of his mouth as red as the lipstick in a Marilyn Monroe poster.

Betel nut is the 'poor man's beer', a mild narcotic chewed with vigour by men and women alike, sometimes even children, throughout much of Asia and Melanesia. Those bright red splotches are as common to Papua New Guinea and the Solomons as blue sky and coconut palms.

It's a palm too, *Areca catechu*, a spindly-trunked tree with a cluster of green, golden yellow or brownish red nuts hanging well out of reach, perhaps fifty feet in the air, that produces the betel nut.

To the uninitiated, chewing betel nut is about as much fun as getting the 'flu. The results are at first similar, a sort of weak-legged, hot feeling. But ask someone who is used to it and the answer is quite different.

"You feel relaxed," said one, "and you sweat, which makes you cool. It makes you feel happy, just the same as if you'd had two cans of beer."

"The first time you chew it," said another, "you feel a bit dizzy or drunk. But in the villages and at social gatherings, it is the respected thing to do. They will hand betel nut around at the council meetings. People sit quietly talking, their eyes go round, they talk a lot..."

I liked the third account best: "the hot air comes out from your ears and inside, you feel warm and good."

You could grind up all the betel nut in the world and it wouldn't turn red. The red comes from the traditional way it is consumed, namely mixed with powdered lime from the reef, broken coral smashed to a fine powder and dried for a few weeks on a rack over the cooking fire. The final ingredient is a leaf which varies from area to area.

In some parts of Melanesia, quite elaborate tools are part of the custom. Trobriand Islanders incise elegant designs on coconut gourds which serve as lime containers, and carve tiny spatulas out of ebony. In Port Moresby, few Motu-speaking coastal Papuans would be seen in public without their ever-present lime gourds.

Elsewhere, lime containers may be bamboo sections, film cans, tobacco tins or small parcels made up of sago palm leaves.

In the more remote villages, everyone — men, women and children — chew the nut. But the smallest probably aren't mixing it with lime. More often, they're just chewing the outside peel of the nut.

And, unlike fruit, the ripe ones are the hard ones. It takes strong teeth to crack ripe betel nut, so older people go for the green and softer ones.

The more betel nut you chew, and the more quicklime, the brighter red the inside of your mouth goes. And the teeth slowly go coal black. Betel nut chewers are unlikely to win the Colgate Smile poster contract. But what's more important, a beaming ivory smile or hot air coming out of your ears?

Every so often, the government launches another campaign to abolish the custom. It can lead to cancer of the mouth, they say, and the red stains are unsightly. The campaigns aren't very successful. For one thing, village markets sometimes have betel nut and absolutely nothing else to sell, a cash crop which provides a handy income to people who might otherwise have none.

In Honiara, particularly around government offices and civic centres, there are signs warning that chewing betel nut is not allowed. The signs are almost impossible to miss: they're highlighted for several feet all around by a bright red ring.

The I-Kiribati

School children in Titiana Village are rehearsing a song. It's a traditional *I-Kiribati* song, and the children are going through the actions of first seeing a hill, and then climbing it.

It might not seem like a candidate for the Top of the Pops, but for the I-Kiribati living in the Solomons, it's pretty special. Until they got to the Solomons, they'd never seen a hill.

Titiana Village is near Gizo in the Western Province. It, and Wagina at the bottom of Choiseul, are the centres of an all-I Kiribati migration staged by the British administrators between 1958 and 1963. It was a migration which took about 2,500 people from the low-lying Gilbert and Ellis atolls near the Equator — people used to fishing and living from the sea — and dropped them off in lush garden settings where they could maintain a tradition of being absolutely hopeless gardeners.

But the joy of this story is how well this transformation has taken place. The 2,500 or so I-Kiribati in the Solomons are a cultural entity living in what appears to be mutual respect and harmony with their Melanesian hosts.

It actually began before World War II. The Gilbert Islands, said the British, were getting too crowded. So they moved the people to the Phoenix Islands. But then, drought set in and the wells in the Phoenix group became dry or salty. The villagers survived on coconut milk. So the administrators looked around and opted for Gizo and Choiseul, two back-water outposts which, as part of the British Solomon Islands Protectorate, they also administered.

Rev. Ben Taake was nine years old when he boarded the government boat to take him to the Solomons. He came on the second to the last trip, but even then, stories about the fierce, dark-skinned islanders were rampant.

"The first island we saw was Malaita," the Reverend remembers, "and we saw smoke on the hills. People on our boat said Solomon Islanders were cannibals and the smoke meant that they were getting ready to cook us. Others on the boat said the jungle was filled with lions and tigers. Every step we made on shore was a careful one."

"We stopped in Honiara for a while, and I and some other boys my age snuck away. We went to the cinema at Point Cruz, and when we got back to the boat, we were in big trouble. The elders thought we'd been eaten."

"The elders still long to go back. They didn't want to move. We had fish, turtle, birds and coconuts, and parts of the atolls had fresh water. But the administration said we had to move or the lack of fresh water would get worse.

"The Phoenix Islands are isolated now; only devils live there. For the elders, it is still home, but for the young people who were born here in the Solomons, this is home. This is where they want to be."

I-Kiribati customs have remained for the most part intact, not only in their songs and dances, but in their community lifestyles and such things as marriage rituals.

In Titiana and the adjoining I-Kiribati settlements, a girl coming of age may still wear a hand-crafted grass skirt, go without food and water (except coconut milk) for the required three days and, freshly oiled, go out to sweep around the house in a display which is seen by all as an indication of her ripening years. In a really traditional family, grandmother may still insist on softening the grass skirt by chewing it.

Intermarriage, once forbidden, is now more common. And probably half the I-Kiribati community these days wouldn't really expect a girl to be returned to her parents if she failed the white mat test on her wedding day. But then, probably half would. Traditions die slowly here.

Solomon Islanders, says Ben, were the first to break the intermarriage code. "That's nice, nothing wrong with that. I was one of the first I-Kiribati to marry a Solomons girl and now I live in a Melanesian village and I get a little land."

"We were given land when we first arrived, and for the most part, that's the same land we have today. Maybe that's one reason for such good relations: the people here aren't particularly land hungry."

Some of those aspects of living off the sea are peculiarly their own. A style of fishing, a means of calling sharks.

Ben demonstrated the Gilbertese way to fish. It's called *kura*, and it's done by tying a stone with a strap of leaf or coconut frond. A hook with a feather in it is stuck through the end of the leaf strap and gently, both stone and hook are dropped into deep water. A quick tug, the hook pulls free from the leaf and stone, and the feathered jig rises quickly from the depths, an undeniable attraction to some lurking coral cod.

Shark calling, I-Kiribati style, is done by tying clam shells together, or coconut husks on a wire, and rattling them in the sea. The shells crack together with a sound which, for some unknown reason, attracts sharks. Sometimes the fishermen make a wire hoop big enough for the sharks to swim through. Sometimes, they use a sizable hook, baited with a bonito, the line tied to the canoe. If it isn't a Nantucket sleigh ride, it's at least a Gizo bobsled.

And they make toddy. Hardly anyone else seems to bother, although plenty of Solomon Islanders like *drinking* toddy.

One of the best initial contacts for the I-Kiribati in Gizo is Ron Parkinson, a self-made expert on their affairs for the simple reason he takes tourists to all their villages and has painstakingly learned all the questions visitors are likely to ask.

The only problem with Ron is finding the 'off button'. En route on his visits, he stops his truck every twenty feet, an on-going oration on vegetation, birds, useful plants, mat-making, and the best place to find the villagers if they happen to be in town.

Nusa Babanga, an offshoot village alongside Titiana, was in the midst of a Chinese Checkers game with quite a number of spectators. Among them, feet hanging over a porch railing, was 20 year old Tarie. He'd finished Fifth Form at a mission school in New Georgia but didn't have much luck finding a job in Honiara.

He has mixed emotions. He'd like to find a job. But he doesn't want to miss out on his village lifestyle, life the I-Kiribati way.

Spirits of Roviana Lagoon

For two of the people in the boat, it was their first ocean dive. They'd finished their PADI training sessions and they were about to plunge into the very blue water of Roviana Lagoon.

The dive boat was anchored not to the bottom, since the bottom was 500 metres down, but to the overhanging branches of Tomba-Tuni Island, perched mid-lagoon on the tip of an extinct volcano a few miles out of Munda.

There's a Solomon Islands tourism poster which depicts a painted island and a profusion of undersea colour, and it reads 'As beautiful above as it is below'. Sitting on the dive boat waiting for the divers to re-emerge, the forty minutes they were down went by in what seemed a moment's meditation. Almost before the regulator was out of their mouth, the young couple from Wales were launching into an animated description of the wonders of their new world...eagle rays, turtles, a wall of soft corals and gorgonians.

Breathless more from oratory than diving, Rob and Claire had just become the latest converts to one of the Solomons' biggest attractions. And they'd chosen Munda for their adventure, with Solomon Sea Divers, based at Agnes Lodge.

Dave and Marianne Cooke accepted the offer to run the dive operation there, sight-unseen. They'd just completed PADI instructor courses in Australia and neither of them was suffering from wanderlust. Dave had been trekking through Asia, India, Nepal and Africa (he met Marianne in Capetown) and together, they'd wandered around in Zimbabwe and Malawi, gone back to Dave's home in England, then gone on to Thailand, Singapore and Australia.

Without knowing what they were in for, they signed on to work in Munda. 'What they were in for' being what must be one of the most pristine, island-surrounded, clear-water lagoons anywhere: traffic jams of sometimes two boats in the channel at once, a relaxed pace of life and Rendova peak climbing out of the clouds as a perpetual reference point. Tough life. They began selecting their dive spots.

Since nobody had dived commercially there, that was accomplished by asking the local boys "where do you see the most fish...unbroken reef... sharks?" And they'd go off for a look.

After an elderly villager told them about a huge Liberator, a World War II bomber which supposedly had nose-dived into Roviana near Rendova, they spent countless hours searching for the wreck. Instead, they found what they call the most beautiful dive spot imaginable, the soft corals protected from cyclones by its location between two islands.

They know where the best gorgonian fans are, where to find large shoals of barracuda and other pelagics, where the eagle rays and sharks will be, along with all the other residents of the reef, the parrotfish and Maori wrasse and surgeonfish.

For the war buffs, there's a Japanese freighter, an American

Corsair and a Nell Japanese bomber, the latter apparently the first victory for US air-ace Rex Barber who went on to shoot down Admiral Yamamoto. All of the war relics lie in less than 15 metres of water.

But the Douglas Dive Bomber near Lumbaria Island is special. Villagers first told Dave about the plane in 1991, saying they even remembered the two wartime pilots escaping to shore in a yellow life raft.

Somehow, word of the find reached San Francisco, and a Lt. Dougherty...the plane's pilot. Dave went to San Francisco to meet him, a video and a packet of photographs in hand.

"My plane still sitting there, intact, in the shallow sand seemed unthinkable," Jim Dougherty remarked nostalgically. "The propeller blades still there, the rudder, even my seat. All these years I had no idea..."

Dougherty and his daughter flew to Roviana, the original plan being to let the 75-year-old 'contact' his plane with some pretty sophisticated video equipment as his daughter Candace explored the aircraft and described everything she could explain.

Jim wouldn't hear of it. He wanted to go down himself, wanted to touch his plane, feel the cockpit. He'd never been diving before.

After hurried consultation between dive masters and a visiting TV crew, it was agreed. Jim was pretty darn fit and he should have the opportunity to go down if he wanted to.

On July 23, exactly 52 years to the day when the dive bomber hit the sea, Jim was sitting in his cockpit again, giving three worried dive instructors and two dive masters the thumbs up sign.

I'm not a diver. My idea of adventure is to look for something above water, and Dave helped organise a junket to Skull Island.

About an hour away from Munda, the island is a secret little spot that receives very few visitors. It's secret because it's supposed to be. The Rendova people were excellent head hunters in their day, and their chief, Ingave, was apparently the area's champ. When the missionaries started moving in on his trophy case, the villagers moved it to an isolated little island where missionaries were unlikely to venture.

Twenty or thirty skulls decorate the stone-work platform in the centre of the island. Ingave's own skull is there in a little miniature roofed enclosure, and it is surrounded by numerous *bakhia*, large shell-money rings of considerable value. There were three of us in the boat, all of us surprised that, if they were so valuable, nobody tried to steal them.. We asked the guide.

"Somebody could take them," he said. "But their canoe would never reach shore."

Photos taken, skulls and *bakhia* un-touched, we began the journey back to Agnes Lodge. It took four hours instead of one. First we sheared a pin on the outboard's propeller. Enough of the pin lodged in place so that we could go backwards, water lapping over the transom. Then it, too, gave away.

Paddling, we eventually got to Zipolo Habu Island, and somebody there had a spare pin for the prop. The journey resumed.

Why the delay? The only thing I could figure out was that Ingave didn't want his picture taken.

Open Oceans, Open Boat

The man in the red 'long john' top, Greg Blanchette, was sitting at a table in Honiara's Point Cruz Yacht Club. The table was nearly bigger than the open boat he's soloing in, and he was saying that he'd had enough adventures to last a lifetime — and he was only a quarter of the way around.

Those adventures included close encounters with whales, being de-masted on a Mexican reef, and turning upside-down twice in mid-ocean. And then there were the adventures of the mind, the fits of depression caused by extreme solitude, living in a shell with a roof that is only eighteen feet long.

The people at the Yacht Club were looking at the tiny green boat with the Maple Leaf flag and suggesting that Greg must be, you know, a bit nuts. Out of his head. They were the people who hadn't had a chance to meet him yet, who hadn't discovered that 37-year-old Blanchette was sane enough to be frightened, a soft-spoken adventurer in awe of 'the way things seem to work, the poetry of facing an unbroken hemisphere of sky.'

"Back home," he said, "I always felt I was living behind a glass wall, insulated and distracted. In mid-ocean, everything is so simple: water, food, doubt and life. That's when you get your glimpse of poetry, when you are most strongly touched by small things."

Poetry, maybe, but some of it is of the darkest kind. Long, frustrating passages, visions of death, wet and turbulent days afloat questioning the motives behind the mission.

Blanchette has embraced adventure before. He has bicycled through the Middle East, gone kayaking in the Arctic, gotten down to grips with nature. But this venture is certainly the most ambitious. He says he knows of three other efforts to sail around the world in an open boat, but none made it.

He left Vancouver in September, 1991, late enough in the season that he decided to forego sea-trials and 'learn how she handled on the way.' He kept a low profile, not even alerting newspapers of his plans, worried that the US Coast Guard would stop him under a 'Manifestly Unsafe Voyage' clause. They did stop him, and they debated for some time whether to let him continue. A lone man without an engine or radio transmitter, at sea in something little bigger than a canoe. But the British-built Drascombe Lugger has a look of being seaworthy, there were safety flares and 90 litres of water aboard, and Blanchette convinced them he was just sailing down the coast to Mexico to get warm and have a few *cervezas*.

Have a good trip, they said.

The passage south, his first open water, was 'scary as hell' because he kept anticipating storms, watching cloud sheets from the north which usually meant rough weather. The storms didn't materialise.

Triangle Island (his boat is named for a very small, windswept island off Vancouver) kept her nose pointing toward warmer climes.

Just off the coast of Mexico, he was writing in his log book "haven't seen any whales and I wonder why" when he watched in horror as a big broil of water right under the boat got bigger and bigger. "I was right on top of migrating humpbacks, and I started jumping up and down, banging the bottom of the boat to say 'I'm here, I'm here.' Later, with whales all around, he would hang a battery-operated strobe light over the side to warn them off.

The plan was to reach the end of Mexico's Baja Peninsula and turn right toward Hawaii. But *El Nino* was causing havoc with the weather and there were storms everywhere. Greg decided to go as far south as Cabo San Lucas, and then head across. Midway along the coast, he sailed into a secluded bay and hit a reef, breaking both masts. Disaster so soon? But there were lobster fishermen in the bay and they towed the boat in. For two weeks, while the new masts were being shaped and fitted, Blanchette ate lobster and tortillas. The good life.

Five days back at sea, still en route to Cabo, *Triangle Island* surfed down a wave sideways and rolled over. Greg was thrown free, climbing back aboard on what was now the keel. The 18-foot, nine-inch lugger, according to the specifications, would not be able to be righted, single-handedly, at sea.

"But I didn't have any choice," Blanchette said. "I found a line, pulled like hell and slowly she came over, still filled to the gunwales." It took a lot of bailing. Fortunately, the supplies — food, water, tools and charts — were all in water-tight lazarettes and nothing was lost to the sea. It was a terrifying experience.

Two days later, it happened again.

Blanchette installed 'flip ropes' like a white-water raft.

The passage from Cabo to Hawaii was frustratingly long. The sleeping space, a coffin-shaped slot in the tiny well between centreboard and lazarette, was less than comfortable. Sitting became an ordeal, so much so that his log entries referred to the 'dead zone'. Each morning, pushing aside the plastic tarp which reflected some of the salt spray, he surveyed the day over a bowl of corn flakes and powdered milk. There is no stove of any kind aboard, no fuel or means of heating food.

Books (only one of them on sailing) carried because "they were ones I thought I should read" were so boring they nearly drove him crazy. He began inventing little things to do, like sewing a wallet out of a piece of torn sail. He played the mouth organ until only three notes were still recognizable: salt water had etched the rest of the metal reeds away. He sang to himself, loudly. The little Sony Walkman wasn't much good away from civilisation, but occasionally picked up snatches of another world.

"I learned patience" he said, in what must be one of the understatements of the year. "Loneliness isn't a problem, but solitude is. You feel so vulnerable." Little things began to bug him, the self-steering lines snagging his elbow, an unexpected splash of salt spray. Blanchette confessed that, several times, he got so mad he just raged into the darkness, swearing at everything. And then he'd take control again.

Crossing the Tropic of Cancer, there was a bang on the transom and a new hole in the rudder where a shark had bitten it. During an almost windless day, he hopped over the side to scrape sea-weed off the hull and stared in amazement at a billfish plummeting toward him. He scrambled back aboard, hands protecting his rear.

The landfall, finally, in Maui was a physical and psychological relief. He flew home for a spell, reassuring his parents and friends that he was OK. "They're philosophical about my wanderings" said Greg, "but they're always glad to hear from me. Friends just say, Oh, here we go again."

En route from Hawaii to the Solomons, there were no near-disasters. "Mishaps are catchier and more colourful than the real stuff of a voyage," the sailor said. From Tarawa to Honiara, the 'real stuff' was too little wind, too much rain. Greg got a bit casual about food supplies, finally having to make do with mashed potato flakes mixed with jam, a tin of tuna with soy sauce. Thankfully, on a boat with no stove, he likes cold beans.

Gray skies and rain kept him from getting an accurate sextant sight, sometimes for days. There is no sophisticated satellite navigation rig. Just a sextant, watch and compass. Still, he manages to "come in pretty close to where I'm supposed to be."

Near the south coast of Malaita, the breeze dropped off altogether. Triangle Island, which on some days had averaged a nice 100 miles, was suddenly going nowhere. Fifteen miles a day, now nine. And then halfway to Santa Cruz, it began drifting backwards.

Greg began rowing. For eight days, he could see the same land.

Greg Blanchette reached Honiara on June 14, 1993, twenty-one months after he left Vancouver.

Darwin, Bali, Singapore, the Straits of Malacca, the Indian Ocean and Red Sea, France and the stormy Atlantic crossing to the East Coast of Canada lay ahead. A lonely and ambitious undertaking.

He is acutely aware of the pirates in the China seas. "Maybe," he says hopefully, "I'll be too small to see."

In Honiara, surrounded by a growing number of admirers, he met and told his story to all sorts of people. He spent his days ashore, his nights on the boat, despite invitations to make use of a comfortable bed.

For some unexplained reason, he didn't seem comfortable sleeping out of sight of his lady, his Drascombe lugger.

Calling the Herons

John Hunuratana Iuhanakahu can call the herons.

In Malaita, that is the same thing as saying he can catch a thief. He can also tell villagers whether or not they should undertake sea voyages, cross flooded rivers safely, or swim in estuaries which are known crocodile territories.

John can tell a pregnant woman whether she should expect a boy or a girl.

Call it magic if you like, but John doesn't use that word.

He says it is an ancestral form of Melanesian divination, and the 74-year-old Nariora Villager, from West Are' Are', is known from one end of Malaita to the other for his powers of perception.

I met him in Honiara when he was visiting his son, John Naitoro, at the National Art Gallery. Being on the former premises of the Governor General wasn't anything new to John senior — he was a former policeman and guard at the residence years ago. But what was handy was having his son, a trained anthropologist, translate the tales of John Hunuratana Iuhanakahu's talents.

When someone in a village suspects someone else of stealing his pig or his wife or his bush knife, they call John. He calls the herons, in the last incident three of them, which sat on the roof of a man's house for three days until he admitted his guilt.

The rituals for custom marriages and the recitations which go with them are almost forgotten now. Who do you call? J.H.I. He can also help pregnant women with problem deliveries, and as a pharmacist of custom medicines, he has the vines, plants and leaves to cure everything from hemorrhaging to tuberculosis.

The techniques are not learned, he says. They are inherited.

Once, a few years back, a family member was having a problem with a 'peeping Tom'. Old John put some heavy-duty hex on the area behind the house, warning the family at the same time that they mustn't go out there until he'd removed it.

But someone in the family wanted to see for himself, walked behind the house, and got zapped by an airborne 'blue electric spark' which knocked him unconscious. He revived, of course, no doubt with a little better idea of what the hex could do.

In Malaitan tradition, good and bad have the same 'weight'. There is no hierarchy of good spirits over bad. I know this because J.H.I. told me so.

Thus, interpreting the signs is a valuable skill in the village. Not black magic, but a case of custom knowledge working in ways few of us will ever understand.

Eat a Croc

Sitting in a back-water pub some time back, an ex-crocodile shooter turned crocodile farmer was explaining some remarkable things about these reptilian behemoths.

Crocodiles can slow their heartbeat down to four beats a minute, for instance. And the egg temperature during incubation determines whether most of the newborn crocs will be male or female. Change the temperature a few degrees and, presto, change the sex.

Quite remarkable. But then it's a little hard to find something about crocodiles which isn't remarkable. Anything that grows up to look that big and that mean is a creature to contend with.

Just underneath those murky, muddy waters, homing in on your thigh as you blithely wade across a jungle tributary, a 12-footer is about to have you for dinner.

What an abominable thought. Far better for you to have *him* for dinner, although this is a most unconservation-like attitude.

But eating croc is one of Papua New Guinea's many cultural experiences, something to write home about, and what's even more important, it's really quite delicious.

The best place to be *eaten* by crocodiles is probably the Sepik, the Fly River, or maybe one of the many little rivers flowing out to sea from the Gulf District. There are fresh water crocodiles inland, saltwater crocodiles in the sea, so you have a reasonably good selection to choose from.

One of the best places to *eat* crocodiles is the Kokoda Trail Motel, about 40 km from Port Moresby on the Sogeri Plateau. Having crocodile steaks on a skewer here has the added benefits of a beautifully scenic drive up the Sogeri Gorge on a paved road, and being in the same area as Rouna Falls and the Varirata National Park.

In fact, it's such a good combination, that a lot of Port Moresby-ites do this for weekend entertainment. Wander the park, down a beer or two at the Bluff Inn en route, and glomp a croc.

Barbequed and on a skewer, it is a firm white meat with a rich, sweet taste. For some reason, it also has a bit of a rich smell, not offputting to true gourmets who eat a lot of things, cheeses among them, that are aromatically detectable.

On quiet weekdays, the motel doesn't always have crocodile on the menu, but on weekends, it's there for sure.

The road up, incidentally, passes alongside Moitake Wildlife Centre, which has lily-clad ponds filled with crocodiles of all sizes. Feeding time is on Fridays, and a local chap hangs out over the pond to dangle a chicken or two over the placid pond.

What emerges out of that water, at lightning speed, is positively frightening. Flying teeth, the grin saying monsters lurk where chickens fear to tread. Or something like that.

But Papua New Guinea, you remember, is culturally strong on the notion of payback. Just remember, the next time you're wading gulf tributaries, you ate a crocodile. So, in fairness...

A Beach Awash: Waikiki

It's probably the most famous beach in the world, a perpetually people-packed strip of latter-day Polynesia which beckons thousands of visitors daily; a potpourri of cultures integrated by a common costume with beach mats and their community flag.

On a fine day, the heady aroma of suntan oil wafts above Waikiki thicker than fog in a Boston winter.

In Hawaiian, Oahu is said to mean 'the gathering place', but it is a tiny section of Oahu, a mere fraction of the city and county of Honolulu, that funnels and siphons the flow.

Nine out of ten of Hawaii's visitors spend at least their first night in Waikiki. When the couple from Centreville, USA, say they are going to Honolulu, they do not mean that executive, businesslike seat of City and State Government which in its tidiness and efficiency manages to carry on, totally unperplexed by the party going on in the back yard. What they mean to say is that they are going to Waikiki.

And in all truth, there's no place quite like it.

Waikiki is a daily carnival, a forever-festive display of the human creature and all its passions: joggers, health fanatics, honeymooners, gold beach boys, fish-belly-white New Yorkers who've traded snow storms for *muumuus* and mai tais; people with trim waists and long legs; the bikini-clad and surf-mad; street walkers and talkers, sun worshippers and fun worshippers seeding in on all that Waikiki offers, from Polynesian spectaculars to porno shops.

And all under the guise of dipping their toes in the most trod-on sand in the world, bathed in the makings of the golden Hawaiian tan.

Even in ancient times, the beach was a favourite surfing place of Hawaiian royalty. Royalty gradually moved out as an ever-increasing influx of visitors moved in, particularly after the taro patches, rice paddies and swamps of the pre-1920s were filled in.

For sure, some sophisticates wouldn't be caught dead heading for Waikiki. There are scores of seasoned travelers seeking seclusion and hidden retreats. But, despite the crowd, maybe even partly because of it, thousands more love it.

My Honolulu - oops - Waikiki day begins with a squint out of the curtained window of my hotel room. The sun is emerging over Diamond Head. The sky is blue. As usual. It never ceases to amaze me that, when it does rain here, it conveniently seems to do it between 3 and 4 in the morning, just enough to keep the air fresh and the grass green.

I am not particularly intrigued with macadamia-nut pancakes, but two or three cups of good Kona coffee is a powerful starter. There are already people on the beach at first light, and of course the joggers are padding the turf at Kapiolani Park with the zeal of a Flemington trotter on Cup Day. There are reportedly more runners per capita in this neck of the woods than anywhere else in America, which makes a certain amount of sense, considering the joys of running in, say, an Idaho blizzard.

It is time to observe the passing parade along Waikiki's main drag, Kalakaua Avenue.

Across the street, or to be more precise, across the street for three solid blocks, is a string of Japanese tourists who are artfully following the bright orange, helium-filled balloon of their tour leader in the far distance. Package tours are big business in this country...some of the bigger Japanese consortiums even foot the bill for a mass holiday or honeymoon, just to ensure that all their employees take their leave at the same time. It is a demure, exceptionally polite attack force, the grandchildren of the Zero pilots who crossed the leeward ranges more than fifty years ago.

Almost everybody in the passing parade is worth a closer scrutiny: the five-year-old kids on bicycles with mini-boards strapped across their handlebars; the islander wearing a 'Hawaiian — Endangered Species' T-shirt; the fellow in wet-suit and full diving gear with a metal detector under his arm. Beach attire, including the G-strings that could grow into bathing suits, seem to be as acceptable on the Avenue as they are on the beach, which is one reason people-watching is such a delight.

Young America is lean, tanned and fighting fit.

There are plenty of trendy shops to wander into, but I am not in the market for Gucci bags, designer jeans, or even scrimshawed whales. Which isn't to say I don't at least enjoy a wander through the International Market Place, that vine-hung, banyan-tree shaded circus of supper clubs, Boom Boom rooms, portraitists, and 'get your picture with a parrot' backdrops, all sheltering under a myriad of fairy lights and Japanese lanterns.

After all, a carnival is a carnival. But when it comes to shopping, I, like countless thousands of other visitors, am wooed away from the beach just long enough to experience the Ala Moana Shopping Center, where I can find some of America's true-blue bargains...good, durable leisure-time sports wear, hiking boots, inflatable boats, artistic books, all the things I can't seem to find back home.

The bus fare to the Ala Moana is the same bus fare to anywhere else on Oahu, including even the three-hour round the island jaunt. Riding The Bus is probably Hawaii's best travel bargain, and the bus drivers endure the tourism onslaught tolerably well. Considering that one out of two passengers has to ask 'Is this the bus to...", a question daily multiplied times one thousand, only the most mild-mannered drivers survive.

Those same buses carry the enlightened *malihinis*, the newcomers, to other destinations around the island: to Makapuu Beach, Sea Life Park, the Polynesian Cultural Center, and a score of surfing beaches where only the wary and bonafide water-people dare tread.

But I am not leaving Waikiki. It is afternoon. The sun is hot and the minuscule bikinis are undulating shoreward, a heart-warming sight.

My favourite day on the beach is Saturday, the day the locals come out to play. Across from the zoo on the Diamond Head side of the hotels, frisbee players, gymnasts, flautists, flauntists, Hare Krishnas and a wonderful entourage of power-to-the-people drum beaters pound out a tempo that has the rest of the beach audience for fifty yards around, body tapping on their beach mats.

And just when the magic is working best, a lion roars. No, not a figment of the imagination, but Honolulu Zoo which is a relaxing break after a day of studying *Homo Sapiens*. A giraffe's head leers over the foliage as a white-handed gibbon scampers out of reach from a playful swat of a crocodile tail. The zoo is just one of the goodies Waikiki *leis* on; others include a military museum, Kodak-sponsored hula show, concerts in the park, most of them free.

For the more robust, I can recommend the hike which begins in the centre of Diamond Head's crater and winds its way 760 feet up the inside wall to overlook all of Waikiki and the rest of Honolulu below. There are spooky dark tunnels and more concrete stairs than some shaky knees can endure, but the war-time bunkers on top are certainly a room with a view.

Just thinking about the climb is enough to bring on a thirst. One of the most intriguing and hospitable drinkeries in town is the Rose and Crown, a Tudor-styled English pub with memorabilia a-plenty on the walls and a piano banger guaranteed to tear songs out of the rustiest, ale-parched throat. The Rose and Crown quickly fills with people after sunset, but the camaraderie is worth the jostle.

For those wanting candle-light intimacy without the menagerie, take heart. Decide what you want and, in Waikiki or greater Honolulu, it is there, be it blush of empress shrimp, medallions of venison, sushi or Maui catfish.

There are sky-high restaurants with prices to match, wharf-side eateries with live lobsters and steamed clams waiting to garnish your drawn butter; ultra-exclusive dens where Mumm's the word, or sit-anywhere bistros featuring plate lunches of taro and kalua pig, Mexican munchies, sukiyaki, something yuckie. In short, whatever you want for however much you want to pay.

My favourite would have to include the Spaghetti Factory, a Tiffany-lamped Victorian-furnished, totally inexpensive choice for a business lunch or companionable dinner, providing spaghetti in one form or another, coupled with fresh salads and platters of hot sour-dough bread are welcome to your palate.

And there are a number of good, inexpensive steak houses where a slab of prime beef and a cold bottle of Bud costs less than the hors d'oeuvres in some trendier dining spots.

After dark, Waikiki goes bananas. Everybody is on holiday; everybody for at least two weeks out of the year, is having every night out. It's what they dreamt about all those nights while watching Hawaii-Five-O on the tube, and now, by heaven, they're going to do it. From bouzouki to bluegrass, from amateur strip night at the Lollipop to sultry lips and undulating hips of the Polynesian reviews, it's show time and the show frequently carries on until dawn.

But if songsters, swooners or stand-up comedians aren't your cup of tiny bubbles, there is more in the offing. Top entertainers hit the nightspots of Honolulu as if it were a natural extension of Vegas, and the list of attractions drops from there, right down to the 25-cent peep shows in the girlie arcades.

In earlier days, it was Chinatown's opium dens, wild bars and wilder women that lured the sailors in from the seven seas, but these days, Waikiki has its colourful side, too. "Want a date?" is the opening gambit of the high-heeled swingers who hit Kalakaua at sunset, working on the premise that nobody should be lonesome on their holiday.

Waikiki is tireless, a non-stop party that draws some of its revelers back year after year after year. It is part of the Great American dream, as American as apple poi.

A Knife for the Heart

I was supposed to be writing a story about road trains, those 44-wheeled mega-trucks that lumber across the parched Australian bush between Darwin and Adelaide, humping four or five trailers in a line at fairly unbelievable speeds. The dust clouds they kick up are visible from miles away. Except torrential spring rains in Queensland had flooded every low-lying part of the State and the parched Australian bush wasn't parched at all. It was drowning in mud thicker'n stringy-bark gum and there wasn't a dust cloud in sight.

I had an air fare to Townsville, and, according to the plan, I was supposed to find my own way to 'the centre' and link up with the first road train on the 'Ghan that would stop for my waggling thumb. Except I couldn't seem to get out of Townsville, because of the floods. And the dollars I'd allowed myself to create this story were disappearing fast. Day after day of unrehearsed Townsville living.

With just enough left for one more counter-tea and two more beers, I was beginning to panic a little bit.

Not much I could afford to do, either, besides walk around the town's perimeter and look in shop windows.

One of those windows belonged to a hardware store. And inside, along with the Dubbin and dingo baits, saddles, axe handles and tins of paraffin, was a knife.

Nice knife, too, and expensive. I knew, because I had its identical twin back in my pack in the hotel room. A Buck sheath knife which had set me back more than a hundred dollars when I bought it years earlier in Papua New Guinea.

The knife in this hardware store had a tag on it reading $130. And without being quite sure what I intended to do, I raced back to my room, grabbed my Buck and returned to the hardware. My knife didn't look quite as pristine as the one in the shop: it had opened a few too many tough betel nuts, prised open several cans, and the sheath was, well, a little abused, too.

I waited.

Maybe an hour later, a four-wheel-drive 'ute' pulled up in front of the hardware. No paint left on it. A wire cage in the back with four or five Blue Heelers in it. The driver got out, all beard and blue singlet.

"Scuse me, mate," I said. "See that Buck knife in the window? Well, I got the exact same one, but I need to sell it, and you can have mine for thirty bucks."

The beard yelled for his dogs to stop growling, and then he looked at my knife and he looked at the one in the window. "That'll be right" he said.

And he opened his wallet and paid me one hundred and thirty dollars.

I damn near cried, I was so astonished. But you don't cry in front of a bush Queenslander. He'd think you were a bloody poofter. So I said thanks, and said I was trying to get out of town.

But the roads, you know...

"Take a train," he said. "The goods train oughta be heading to Isa in a couple of hours."

And with my pack and $130 dollars in my pocket, that's how I got on the 8:41 to Cloncurry.

The 'goods train', a freight train back where I come from, was sitting at a siding right where the man with the ute and the dogs and the Buck knife said it would be. And yes, said the guard, it was leaving soon. West. "Could I catch a lift" I asked, explaining all the problems I'd had getting out of Townsville after the rains.

"Don't see why not" he said, and pointed to the last car in the line, the caboose, although Queenslanders probably don't call it that.

Whoopee, after days of being stationary, I was about to go nipping down the line, heading for the Northern Territories and my story on territory truckies.

We left as dusk softened into dark, the guard barely acknowledging my presence, the train moving. Any resemblance between this and Japan's bullet train is purely coincidental, I thought, but it was moving. Lurching, sort of.

I slept. And with daylight came the changes in countryside I had anticipated. The blue gums and stringy-barks, the land drying up considerably, the haze that pulsated in shimmering layers just over the hard-packed surface.

I was getting a little hungry and the guard didn't seem inclined to offer anything from his tin box of goodies, but what the heck: surely we'd stop in a town soon.

But we didn't.

Every time we approached civilisation, we rumbled through it. When we did finally stop, a procedure that was getting to be monotonous, it was on a siding in the middle of nowhere, a three or four hour wait without any apparent reason. Sometimes another goods train went past the other way. Sometimes it didn't.

Hours of perching in the shade alongside the guard's car, swatting flies, studying an anthill, counting the grease-slicked stones in the siding, the number of timber sleepers countable before they dissolved into the horizon.

I slept. During the night, the train moved somewhat. By morning, I was fiercely hungry. Ravenous. There was a different guard, a different lunch-box. His own.

About the time I was thinking of munching road-kills, the dried remains of track-side lizards, the train began to slow. And it was in a town of sorts.

As I leapt, fell, slid down the stairs, a stern warning from the guard: "I shouldn't think we'll be here but a moment or two..."

Oh, bloody perfect: sit in the middle of nowhere for hours and stop in a town for seconds. I didn't care. I had money in my pocket and I could see the white walls of a pub beckoning me across a paddock.

It was closed. It was also a Sunday morning. I banged on the door anyway, and eventually it opened. A short round man with a haystack of pure white hair asked if he could be of service.

It's amazing how speech eludes you when you are trying to blurt out that you've been on a train for days, that you haven't had a bite to eat, that in fact you're damn near starving. And ever so thirsty. I guess some of the message got through, because the fellow said "calm down, lad, just calm down. I'll get the wife to make you up a little something."

And he did. And his wife did. And I was suddenly looking at a wondrous brown bag filled with sandwiches, the bread thick and home-made, still hot and filled with great slabs of mutton, the mustard sliding out between the layers. And six cold cans of beer.

In delirious happiness, I opened my heart and my wallet. No meal could look so good, no beers so tempting.

And then the man with the white hair said "Oh, we don't trade on the Sunday. Just take them. You can look us up if you ever come back this way"... and he closed the door, an Irish saint in Julia Creek.